IMAGINARY

LANDSCAPE

IMAGINARY

MAKING WORLDS

OF

MYTH AND SCIENCE

LANDSCAPE

WILLIAM IRWIN THOMPSON

St. Martin's Press • New York

First published in the United States of America in 1989
Printed in the United States of America

Book design by Robert Bull

ISBN 0-312-02809-1

Library of Congress Cataloging-in-Publication Data

Thompson, William Irwin.
    Imaginary landscape / by William Irwin Thompson.
      p.   cm.
    Includes bibliographical references.
    ISBN 0-312-02809-1: $19.95 (est.)
    1. Cosmology—Miscellanea. 2. Consciousness—Miscellanea.
I. Title.
BF1999.T517   1989
113—dc19   88-31580

CONTENTS

ACKNOWLEDGMENTS

Because *Imaginary Landscape* is most pointedly a work of intellectual friendship, I could not have undertaken or finished this book without the help of others. First, to Mr. William Wood Prince Sr. and the Prince Charitable Trusts of Chicago, I am deeply indebted for the research grants to the Lindisfarne Program for Biology, Cognition, and Ethics that enabled me to work together with Francisco Varela and Evan Thompson in Paris in association with Varela's color vision laboratory at the University of Paris VI. That Mr. Wood Prince was also willing to participate in the Lindisfarne conference at the Centro Luigi Bazzuchi in Perugia that explored the implications of the Gaia hypothesis as a basis for design, made the intellectual friendship that is basic to this book one of the most memorable events of my life.

I am deeply indebted to Francisco Varela and to my son, Evan Thompson, for reading and providing detailed suggestions for improving the manuscript as I wrote and rewrote it during the winter and spring of 1988. By allowing me to read their work in progress, *Worlds Without Ground,* I was able to understand that cognitive science is not a threat to philosophy or the humanities, but, in fact, a new way for the academic humanities to be more human and less academic.

To my daughter, Hilary, I am indebted for a wonderful afternoon of research at the library of Trent University in Ontario, when we roamed through the stacks of reference books, as if they were trees in Grimms' forest, looking for Rapunzel. It was Hilary who unearthed Anton Kerner von Marilaun's wonderful *Natural History of Plants* (London, 1895) that confirmed our Irish hunches by giving us the story of autogamy and showing us a drawing of the pistil with its collecting hairs. Mothers and daughters have their ancient mysteries, but in the search for lost cosmologies in the light of the future, it is comforting to know that fathers and daughters as well can discover a new kind of intellectual magic.

Lynn Margulis and James Lovelock generously gave of their time in reading my material about them, and joining us for the gathering in Perugia that explored the cultural implications of their work. I have learned so much from the two of them that I have almost forgotten what it was like when I did not have their ideas in my head.

And to Andra Akers and her institute in Los Angeles and Santa Fe, Synergy International, I wish to express my profound gratitude for introducing me to Ralph Abraham, sending me his books, and making sure that the two of us had time to meet and perceive what she had seen at once: that our minds were living just around the corner from one another in one of Italo Calvino's imaginary cities and we just had to meet and become good neighbors. "Gaian Cosmologies," in an earlier version, first appeared in *IS Journal,* Vol. 2, No. 2, December 1987, along with Ralph Abraham's "Mathematics and Evolution: A Proposal" and "A Conversation with Francisco Varela." Through her institute and its *IS Journal,* Andra has helped all of us who are looking for new ways for artists and scientists to overcome the split of "the two cultures" and begin to work together toward the realization of a new planetary culture.

To my editor at St. Martin's Press, Kermit Hummel, I wish to express my deep gratitude for his belief in this book, long before there was anything resembling the length of a manuscript that could justify such good faith; and for working with me, chapter by chapter, as I tried to understand just what it was I was looking for in this new genre of *Wissenskunst.* Europe still holds to literary traditions that allow poetry, the literary essay, and philosophy to keep good company, but it is not easy to find, in the hard and commercial world of New York publishing, editors who can sympathize and understand that breaking the rules together, like the breaking of bread, can also be a staff of life.

PROLOGUE

IMAGINARY LANDSCAPE WITH FOUR FRIENDS THINKING APART

THE IMAGINATION IS AN ANCIENT FACULTY, PER-
haps so ancient that it even antedates the origins of language
and comes out of a lost time when sight could hear space
shudder and smell could sense the interpenetration of each in
all. So universal and encompassing is this faculty of mind that
we single out as creative or crazy those peculiar individuals
who persist in thinking in images. It would be poetic to think
that the creative imagination is only the realm of the archaic
mind of religion and art and survives, like a Hopi Mesa lifted
above the suburban cities of the Arizona plain, with an am-
bivalent mixture of encroachment and indulgence in the middle of our scientific and technical world. But it is also in the
science of creative individuals that we come upon this peculiar
habit of making discoveries through a quiet reverie in which
the image floats to the surface of the chaotic stream of data.
Normal scientists who willingly restrict themselves to the rou-

tines of their bureaucracies do not seem to be open to this more contemplative form of thought, but like postal clerks they are happy to stamp received opinions and pass them on. Creative scientists, however, seem more shaman than priest, and their mode of thinking does not differ greatly from the composer or the poet.

Sickly, young Descartes, permitted by the priests to stay in bed after the other children had arisen and gone to class, could stare at the ceiling and see his thoughts. Out of that habit of visual thinking, analytic geometry developed, and out of that visual imagination came Descartes's dreams, his meditations, and his almost gnostic myth of the evil demiurge of the deceiving spirit.

Exalted on a peak in the Andes, Darwin saw how we were all netted together; raging in a fever, A. R. Wallace saw the lineaments of the theory of evolution. It is much the same process when Kékulé dreamed of the benzene ring or Glaser stared at the bubbles in his glass of beer and saw the bubble chamber for particle physics he went on to invent.

The time when the image or geometrical figure is still implicit and has not yet surfaced on the stream of data is the intuitive moment, the unsettling instant when an itch is just maddeningly beyond the reach of scratch and one feels that one has to stretch to new lengths to reach it. But all the stretching and nervous scratching never seems to get at it; then comes the surrender, the release, the moment of profound, contemplative quiet, and there, floating like a standing wave in a turbulent stream, it appears. Poincaré gave up looking for the solution to the theorem, and then, casually as he lifted his foot to alight on a tram, the solution flashed into his thoughts. When the image is not simply a solution to a problem but to an entire theory, as it was when Crick and Watson imaged the double helix of the DNA molecule, then the shape changer of the thought changes the shape of science.

We are now at another one of those historic moments when a scientific itch is just beyond the reach of scratch, and it is a particularly maddening time, especially for those who stand outside the sciences in the humanities and can only sense what they cannot know. For those of us who lack the mathematical tools and scientific knowledge to articulate what they intuit, one sane way to compensate for our individual inadequacies is to think in an ensemble devoted to a kind of intellectual chamber music, or, perhaps, it would be better to consider it a more informal kind of mind-jazz that through theme and variation seeks to explore the limits of the given mentality of the historical epoch. The crazies are those unfortunate souls who lack sensitive companionship and consequently pop, like an astronaut without a space suit, to create their own private universe in which they try to play all the instruments in the ensemble at once to become both performance and audience to themselves. Lacking a culture or even a subculture, they have the bad luck to be completely alienated and alone, and that is enough to drive anyone mad, for humans are inherently culture-bearing animals and cannot experience their humanity without the appropriate language and culture.

Sometimes when one intuits new ideas, or perhaps even a new world view, and these intuitions are not shared by one's colleagues, it becomes necessary to leave one's professional situation to seek out the true colleagues of that emergent intuition. In 1967 when I was a young assistant professor of humanities at MIT, I began to feel that the postindustrial culture of the leaders of MIT, as well as the leaders of the ruling institutions of the postwar world, was inadequate and, perhaps, even an incorrect interpretation of our actual historical situation. Since MIT was the Vatican of this postindustrial society, I decided to quit and to begin a search for my true colleagues in the emergence of what I felt was "a new planetary culture."

At MIT, there was no thought of planetary culture as anything but the spread of MIT's intellectual domination into all fields and cultures. Although I did not meet Humberto Maturana at that time, I did meet his colleague Jerome Lettvin, and I did observe, from a respectful distance, the great Warren McCulloch as he strolled across the quad outside my window. As a young instructor of humanities watching the battles that were transforming the age of philosophy into the era of cognitive science, I felt like a tiny mammal hiding in the underbrush and watching the great dinosaurs lumbering on by. Warren McCulloch and Noam Chomsky were awesome creatures who were not to be approached.

Jerry Lettvin and Jerry Fodor, however, were amiable, herbiverous sorts of dinosaurs and one could venture safely into their presence, even dare to ask a question, and be treated to an answer, and sometimes even a delightful *yente*'s explanation of what it was all about. The watering hole of the coffee machine in the philosophy department was sometimes safe, but when the Tyrannosaurus Rex of Noam Chomsky appeared, all alien opinions had to scurry to safety in the ferns. There was no question of questioning; there was only the One Truth. If one listened, hidden to the side in the foliage, one could tell how deadly it all was from their language. Conversations, lectures, or presentations were always described as brutal conflicts, and approval was always registered as an act of triumphant violence, such as "I annihilated him." or "He was so stupid as to say x, so I murdered him on the spot." I remember watching Louis Kampf and Noam Chomsky approvingly exchanging expressions of intensely violent language and then, without skipping a beat, go on to discuss the peace demonstration they were about to take part in. Scholarship for them was a form of Ninja assassination, but they still thought that only the hawks in the Pentagon were instruments of domination, violence, and cultural oppression.

There was something dangerous and wrong about this kind of science. When Marvin Minsky proclaimed that the brain was nothing but a computer made out of meat, one could not help but feel that at MIT one was indeed nothing but a piece of meat on the chopping block of analysis. Something was missing, but there was neither space nor time to find out what. One could not expect to find grass and space for rumination in a slaughterhouse; and for a newly arrived and pugnacious Irish-American working-class intellectual from the provinces, the temptation to fall in line with the gang and become as brutal as the big guys was only too attractive. A spiritual approach to the mind was out of the question; the only way to find another way of knowing was to get out and run for your life.

So I left Cambridge, USA, and started to look for people who had a different sense of world culture. I found people like Marshall McLuhan in Toronto, Gregory Bateson, Michael Murphy, and Richard Baker-roshi in California, and David Spangler in Findhorn, Scotland. At first, like so many others of my generation in the 1960s and 1970s, I thought that gurus might have the answer, so I sat at the feet of people like the Mother of Pondicherry or Muktananda. People with turbans such as Gopi Krishna, or with long beards and flowing robes, such as Pir Vilayat Khan, held out a certain exotic fascination, and I thought that they might be the sources of the faint music I was hearing; but, also like so many others of my generation, I found that the gurus were not willing to have sessions in which an intellectual chamber music was possible. They were only interested in giving their one memorized talk over and over again, so I became restless in spirit and less satisfied with "New Age Spirituality." And as the New Age movement advanced into the 1970s, it seemed more and more intent on going backward, until the entire content of its thought was reactionary, both politically and culturally. It wasn't quite what I had in mind, so I found myself, through the friendship with Gregory Bateson, becoming much more interested in scientists of a kind that I had not met at MIT.

When one moves from the academies of philosophy into mind jazz, one never can tell who is going to play in a way that makes a jam session possible. Some people's books are great, but the people themselves are so autistic that they cannot listen to anyone else to shift their own tunes in response or in exploration of new implications of their old patterns of thinking. They have been so isolated in life by their own gifts, and never having found colleagues, they become shaped by adversity into cosmic soloists; but because their gifts are respected, they are not tagged as insane and are accepted as gurus. Both Bucky Fuller and Marshall McLuhan suffered from this kind of cosmic autism and ended up, through multiple recitals of their ideas, becoming holographic tape recordings of themselves. Messiahs to the electronic media, they became its sacrificial victims and showed how the United States dulls bright minds with spotlights. People like Ralph Abraham,* Jim Lovelock;** Lynn Margulis,† and Francisco Varela†† seemed much more open to a kind of intellectual chamber music in which we all learned and changed from playing with one another.

So as the New Age movement began to define the new as paleolithic shamanism, neolithic feminism, pharoahonic architecture, and medieval Islamic geometry, I moved away to stand next to the instrumentalists who were playing new tunes, or new and interesting variations of old ones. It didn't happen all at once, and for a while I was stuck between two stations and was picking up a lot of noise. I was no longer tuned to the MIT of the 1960s, and I was no longer tuned to the holymen and gurus of the 1970s, but I had not yet met the scientists with whom I would work in the 1980s.

That was in 1976, and in 1976, in the grand mystical style of the 1970s I made some predictions about "the return of hieroglyphic thinking" and "the future of knowledge."[1] Even when one makes the right prediction, if one is forced to make

---

* Professor of Mathematics, University of California, Santa Cruz; **Atmospheric chemist, Devon, England; †Biologist, University of Massachusetts, Amherst; ††Neurophysiologist, University of Paris.

---

[1] See "The Future of Knowledge" in *Darkness and Scattered Light* (New York: Doubleday, 1977); also *From Nation to Emanation,* lectures given at Findhorn in 1979 but not published until 1982 by The Findhorn Foundation, Forres, Scotland.

it in a metaphoric language outside the technical language of the specialists who will actually make the discovery, then it still cannot communicate, even if it is published. The lecture I gave *was* published, but the book was shelved in the occult section of bookstores and so it never spoke to the scientists I was actually thinking about. Lacking any knowledge of topology, I had to render my descriptions in the flat forms of a medieval geometry in *From Nation to Emanation* and these diagrams seemed so quirky and occult that they failed to communicate. So I raved on about multidimensional crystals, but not one facet of what I was talking about made sense to any scientist.

When lunatics rave on, they really are trying to say something, but they simply lack the appropriate language. And so it was for all the flat geometries in which I tried to talk about the interpenetration of "Ontos" and "Chaos." What I didn't appreciate at the time, of course, was that prophecy is not prediction but simply an expanded sensitivity to the implications of the present. I wasn't really predicting the future of knowledge, I was simply talking about things that were going on in science in the 1970s that the rest of us would not learn about until the 1980s. What I was thinking about in an ignorant way in the 1970s was also what the mathematicians—the Abrahams, the Smales, the Yorkes, and the Lorenzes—were thinking about at that time in the terms that would come to shape the culture of the 1980s.

Now, thanks to James Gleick's excellent best seller, *Chaos: Making a New Science,*[2] chaos dynamics has become part of the hip counterculture and scientists can once again begin to appreciate the virtues of the visual thinking of the imagination. And there, on the endpapers of Gleick's book, everyone can see Lorenz's strange attractor; but everyone cannot see that W. B. Yeats's double gyre is also there. Yeats's visionary geom-

---

[2] James Gleick, *Chaos: Making a New Science* (New York: Viking, 1987).

etry is esoteric, but not occult and crazy; it is a flat, two-dimensional model for the complex behavior of multidimensional topologies. The double gyre is a metaphor, and metaphors are by their nature *transforms,* stepping down from n dimensions to two or three. Metaphor is, therefore, inescapably the manner in which we humans think, and logical positivism was a waste of time. We are inherently n dimensional beings who have been habituated by a process of fixation *(upadana)* and forgetting *(avidya)* into ignoring all the other dimensions to constitute ourselves in a world *(samsara)* of merely three spatial dimensions. Mystics, prophets, madmen, poets, and mathematicians have tried to deliver us from this prison of our own making, but so unenlightened are we that we rush into the cage, slam the door, and then rattle the bars, screaming to be let out, when, in actuality, there is only a cage in three dimensions, and we are free to leave at will with the right form of mindfulness.

Part of our process of endarkenment is to pose problems that are projections of an inappropriate geometry. People who feel that they are trapped *in,* scream to be let *out;* people who believe that power is at the *top,* struggle to climb *up;* they focus only on the illusionary power of a king or president and fail to understand the chaos dynamics through which a polity behaves and through which a cultural change of directions unfolds without benefit of the directions of a political leader. People who think in terms of centers and peripheries imagine that culture is restricted to institutions like the church or university, and they fail to see the actual creative process through which art, religion, and science reveal themselves in a civilization. Part of the process of enlightenment or discovery is, therefore, the projection of a new geometry that reveals the life of the phenomenon in question, be it Indra's Net or the benzene ring.

We are, again, at one of those exciting times when the creative imagination of an entire civilization is undergoing a transformation of its basic mentality in the shift from one geometry to another. It appears to me that there have been three of these mentalities in Western civilization and that we have now entered the fourth.[3] The first mentality was the arithmetic, the line of counting goods in space and generations in time. This is the mentality of Hesiod's *Theogony* and of *Genesis*. The second mentality is the geometric and it expresses the intellectual revolution wrought by Pythagoras and Plato. For these ancients, motion was imperfect and sinful, and only the unmoving geometry of the perfect spheres in the ideal realm was a true expression of the Good. The third mentality was the dynamic mentality of modernism, the mentality of Galileo, Newton, and Descartes, in which motion and falling bodies became the focus of attention. Now we are moving out of this modernist science with its narratives of linear equations into a postmodernist science of which Chaos Dynamics is one important visual expression. From my external point of view in the humanities, the behavior of these aperiodic phenomena is neither chaotic nor dynamic, and I argued with Ralph Abraham in Los Angeles that these patterns would have been more appropriately called "processual morphologies," and this is the term that I used in *Pacific Shift*. Because I had cut my philosophical teeth in high school on the process cosmology of A. N. Whitehead, I felt that these patterns were only chaotic to a mind restricted to the linear reductionism of scientific materialism, but Chaos Dynamics is the term the scientists have chosen, so the decision has been made and this infant science has been named. Like the Foucault pendulum following its basin and attractor, we do seem to swing from extremes— from technological materialism to New Age psychism, or from a modernist obsession with systems of control to a postmodernist fascination with chaos.

Precisely because we are at the beginning of this shift from the Third Mentality to the Fourth, those who are still in the

---

[3] This is explained at length in "The Four Cultural-Ecologies of the West" in *Pacific Shift* (San Francisco: Sierra Club Books, 1986).

Third are constitutionally incapable of understanding those in the Fourth. If one goes to a scientific conference and watches the two mentalities collide, there is no amount of communication that can get the Third to understand the Fourth. It is like expecting a Prince of the Church in the Renaissance to understand a Galileo or a Descartes.

Impossible, and a waste of time, for what is required is not merely the presentation of data and the communication of ideas, but a metanoia, a shift in the basic mentality in which data is envisioned and articulated. Most people are simply not capable of that kind of radical transformation within a lifetime; as Max Planck said: scientists don't change their minds, they simply die, and younger scientists come along who don't have the old problems of the older generation.

The shift from noia to metanoia requires a change in the structure of world narrative, in the very manner in which a "world" is brought forth. This shift can be a conversion experience for the individual, but for the culture as a whole, the chaos dynamic of consciousness requires a greater nonlinear complexity. If we could sit outside human culture for a while to observe it as extraterrestrials might, we would probably notice that the globality of a civilizational consciousness requires metanoid, paranoid, noetic, and noisy people all interacting at once. Without noise and lunacy, culture would crystallize into a rigid theocracy that would so overproduce the technical monographs of its own sacerdotal trivia that it would generate "a complexity catastrophe" that would all too tragically open up the civilization to the indeterminacies and chaotic instabilities of life. The rigid hierarchy would attract its opposite in the form of an external catastrope, and the civilization would be overrun by primitives or sink beneath Atlantean waves. So a healthier way to preserve the chaotic stability that does not call forth a complexity catastrophe is to tolerate lunacy and noise within the noetic system of the civilization as a whole.

What all this means is that when one is observing one of

these shifts in mentalities, one can learn much from the mystics, crazies, and noisemakers, for they will be performing the new unconscious geometry that no one can yet see. If one is a cultural historian studying the shift in mentalities in the 1970s, then one has to pay attention to popular music, the cults of the drugged crazies, the saner mystics, and the mathematicians, such as Thom, Abraham, Smale, Yorke, and Lorenz, as well as the new biologists, such as Lovelock, Margulis, and Varela.

Looking back on my own association with Abraham, Lovelock, Margulis, and Varela, it seems as if, in my solitude in Bern and my scientific ignorance in the humanities, I constructed an imaginary landscape, a Paul Klee hieroglyph of the illegible, in which I tried to draw out the connections of their works that they themselves could not see or accept. We were not a group and never met as a group, though we all knew one another's work, and yet we formed a cognitive domain and took our dwelling in a planetary culture that was an emergent phenomenon of just that kind of topology that no longer required "simple location" or linear association.

There was Jim Lovelock, the atmospheric chemist living like a poet in an old converted mill in Devon and carrying on, in the best tradition of the British eccentric, as an innovator with the courage of his convictions. He was so gentle of manner, with so soft and musical a lilt to his speech that he seemed more Celt than Saxon, and to listen to him you would never think that he had grown up in Brixton, one of the toughest slums of London. His gentleness, however, seemed to have been learned from hard experience and was the survivor's ability to endure by knowing when to be invisible and when to make an open run for it. Jim had an almost saintly quality of patience and compassion that had deepened in the course of enduring his own illness as well as those of his invalid wife and handicapped son.

Then there was Lynn Margulis, the biologist, his colleague in the articulation of the Gaia hypothesis, but his fiery opposite in temperament. Lynn was an impatient, fast-talking woman of such speed and tightly focused scientific brilliance that only an equal speed, intensity, and mass of hard work could catch her attention and presume to move into orbit alongside her. A lioness of a woman that could raise four children and not only keep up with biology but actually influence its growth, Lynn had strength as well as passion and speed. She had endured a decade of slight and dismissal before her colleagues finally came round to accept her ideas on symbiosis and cell evolution. Like Lovelock from Brixton, she, too, was an underdog and survivor who had, as a Jew in Chicago, worked her way through university and endured all the cruel prejudices the ethnic neighborhoods of that city (which I knew only too well from my own childhood there) could be capable of.

And there was Francisco Varela, the neurophysiologist from Chile, the first of his family ever to attend university. His father had been the last of sixteen sons and the one chosen by the matriarchal grandmother to go down from their tiny mountain village in the Andes to Santiago to become a builder. Cisco grew up in that village in which an intense network of mutual support enabled everyone to survive that rocky solitude, for his father kept his promise to the grandmother and supported the extended family in the village from his work in the city. From that recursive lattice of village and city, individual and family, Varela learned such a profound sense of loyalty to friends that one could feel at ease and accepted in his presence and forget for a moment that he spoke five languages, could lecture in three of them, was as literate in poetry and philosophy as he was in mathematics and science, and that when he wasn't in his neurophysiology lab, he might be found off on a retreat in a Buddhist monastery in Nepal, or playing the flute, or writing poetry in a secret journal that he kept to himself for a decade.

And then there was Ralph Abraham of Santa Cruz, the one I knew the least and was most afraid of, for as I had failed geometry three times in high school, it was precisely geometry and mathematics that had intimidated me all my life. Moreover, Abraham was a wild and California sort of scientist who threw everything into his metahistory, from Teilhard de Chardin to the extraterrestrial syntheses of José Argüelles. His Dionysian and hippie wildness irritated me and upset all my Apollonian canons of discrimination and made me keep my protective distance. Jung maintained that revelation comes through our inferior function: that it takes hold of us where we are most vulnerable and insecure. In no area of human culture am I more ignorant, even stupid, than in mathematics, and yet the transformation of mentality upon which this whole book is based cannot be understood without the new nonlinear, geometrical imagination of Chaos Dynamics. The man I hardly knew proves to be, at the finishing of the book, the one upon whom the whole imaginative landscape depends. Without a new geometrical way of imagining the atmosphere of Lovelock, the planetary microbial bioplasm of Margulis, and the emergent phenomenon of mind "as the organization of the living" of Varela, the work of all three of these scientists suffers and falls back into the fragments of just so much academic data. But with Ralph Abraham's manifestos of "Mathematics and Evolution,"[4] a way is opened to understand how the emergent phenomenon of our new planetary culture is bringing forth new ways of knowing and understanding the atmosphere, the origins of life, and the cognitive domains of the nervous and immune systems.

It was, however, with Francisco Varela in Paris that I worked most closely in thinking all of this out loud in the stimulating noise of cafés and returning home through the whispering tube of the TGV to the protective boredom and

---

[4] See Ralph Abraham, "Mathematics and Evolution: A Manifesto" in *IS JOURNAL* 3 (Los Angeles: December 1986), pp. 28–37. Also "Mathematics and Evolution: A Proposal" in *IS JOURNAL* 5 (Los Angeles: December 1987), pp. 46–65. See also, with Christopher D. Shaw, his *Dynamics: The Geometry of Behavior, Part Three, Global Behavior* (Santa Cruz, Calif.: Ariel Press, 1984).

creative silences of Bern. And it was out of our differing responses, in dream and vision, to Lynn Margulis's films about bacteria that this essay on the imagination began to take shape.

Lovelock, Margulis, and Varela and I all came together for the first time in 1981 for a Lindisfarne Fellows Gathering. But in 1981, I could only see an incoming blip on the Druid radar of my Irish intuition. It was not until 1987, after I had met with Ralph Abraham in Los Angeles in 1985, that I was able to get closer to the shape of things to come. At a dinner with Varela and my son, Evan, in the Alsatian café near Mabillon, I pursued Varela, hoping that he would be able to give a form and a name to the shape changer that had taken possession of me. As had happened before in 1981 when I had enthusiastically babbled about elementals and angels after seeing Margulis's films of bacteria, Varela looked at me with squinty eyes, but when I shifted from words and, in the time-honored, traditional manner, scribbled my intuitions on a napkin, Varela's face changed expression, and his mind began to open to what I was trying to get at. A few months later, and after a few computer run-throughs of his own, he would come up with his own strange attractor for it all.

I asked Varela to consider three separate forms of "operational closure": (1) the assemblage of the first cells in the origins of life (*chez* Margulis), (2) the closure of the immune system he himself had written about and was still working on, a paradoxically open and closed system whose "phase-space" could be seen as "the self," and (3) the emergence of a Gaian dynamic in the atmosphere of the Archaen epoch in which Life, in Lovelock's words, began "to take charge" of the planet to regulate the temperature, the salinity of the oceans, and the oxygen level in the atmosphere. Perhaps "Gaia" was the immune system of the planet and the bacteria that Lynn Margulis studied were its antibodies and lymphocytes. Religious folks anthropomorphized all three of these phenomena with gods because they were thinking in a geometry of center-periphery (actor-acted upon) and irreligious folks reduced it to a linear dynamic that constantly deferred its explanation into another context safely outside the field of their professional concerns. If we could only see that all three of these phenomena were homeomorphs of one another, then perhaps we could come up in our imaginations or computer screens with the right topology or morphology with which we could understand the multidimensional interpenetration of the macrocosm of the atmosphere, the mesocosm of the mind, and the microcosm of the bacteria. We were using the wrong geometry in our imaginations. "What is the shape of the thing I am looking at, damn it!?" I asked Varela as I spiraled around my own scribbles.

And with that question, Varela's face changed; he became silent for only a second, and then he smiled. Finally, I was making sense. But, of course, neither one of us knew the answer, for the answer was rocking in the basin of Abraham.

Bern, Switzerland
June 1988

CHAPTER ONE

RAPUNZEL: COSMOLOGY LOST

1. AT THE THRESHOLD OF THE TEXT

THE HIDDEN GEOMETRY BEHIND EVENTS AS COM-
mon as a dripping faucet or a moving cloud is what the new
mentality of chaos dynamics brings forth.[1] For us moderns, it
is this edge between chaos and order that is most fascinating,
and we search for just the right spot where a momentary stability can provide us with the apparent ground that allows us
to surf-ride the turbulent wave to our personal goal; but as we
stand suspended on that translucent ground, we are given a
moment to see into the groundlessness of all seemingly solid
waves, from the solar system to the circulation of the foam on
the earth's magma that we foolishly call tectonic plates.

For our ancestors, geometry was in a flower or a crystal,
and it was precisely the fixed and unmoving that spoke to

---

[1] See Robert Shaw, *The Dripping Faucet as a Model Chaotic System* (Santa Cruz,
Calif.: Ariel Press, 1983).

them of eternal values in a world of change. The world was chaotic and turbulent enough, and rationality was so infrequent an event in the tragic world of passion and Homeric violence that chaos could not hold out the fascination it now does to our worldwide bureaucracies of routine-operational science. When everything is in flux, it is the not-so-obvious periodicities that capture the imagination of the initiate who begins to perceive the hidden geometry that connects the cycles of the moon or the wanderings of the planets. With the tallying stick of the midwife or the circle of standing stones, the initiate begins to mark out what Gregory Bateson liked to call "the pattern that connects"[2] the singular to the cyclical. Sketched on the sand, the geometry, when seen in the sky, could be seen again in the symmetry of a flower. The image at hand would then be understood to participate in a marvelous system of correspondences of moon and menses, of planets and flowers. "As above, so below" is an axiom of the mystery schools of Thrice Greatest Hermes, but that Alexandrian redaction has its roots in a prehistoric darkness.

Our fairy tales also have their roots in this prehistoric darkness, and the hidden geometry that survives in them is not simply the obvious stuff of phallic symbols and devouring maws but a lost cosmology of correspondences that connect the flowers to the stars. It requires an act of imagination to bring it forth, much in the same way that it requires an act of imagination to look in a new way at the dripping of a faucet.

Precisely because this mythic imagination is no longer valued in our technological culture, and precisely because the prehistoric system of correspondences is indeed lost, I feel that I have to pause before rushing on to unravel a cosmology from a fairy tale. After all, the universities now teach us to deconstruct an author's intended meaning and not to recon-

---

[2] Gregory Bateson, *Mind and Nature: A Necessary Unity* (New York: Dutton, 1979), p. 8.

struct an imaginary lost cosmology from a mere six pages in Grimm. Perhaps if one were to find foreshadowings of Nietzschean nihilism in "Rapunzel," one would be allowed by Jacques Derrida and his school to proceed, but certainly not with the reading I am about to propose, one that reveals no infinite system of deferrals to the void but, rather, the detritus of a prehistoric world view. As this is not the stuff of either modern anthropology or modern literary criticism, one feels the need to pause at the threshold and ask the reader to take a check for her contemporary opinions.

Paradoxically, for my generation, one that came of age in the revolutionary spirit of the affluent 1960s, liberation from institutions and their systems of meanings was not a relationship with a specific oppressive condition but a general, eternal, and absolute value in and of itself. In challenging the rhetoric of Western Civilization, the generation that mocked the bourgeois liberal pieties of its fathers and mothers rather smugly took for granted a naive and simpleminded faith in revolt against all forms of authority and enduring value. And, as always seems to be the case in the world of fashion, the French led the way. Roland Barthes announced "The Death of the Author" and tore down this idol of literate civilization; Michel Foucault exposed the "episteme" that bound institutions and forms of knowing into the "discourse" that was itself the system of domination; and Derrida made certain, with an ultimate Deconstruction, that no text would ever rise up again with a pretense to ultimate meaning, or high-minded and high-handed final authority. For an affluent and expanding bureaucracy of academic literary critics and behavioral scientists, this demolishing of the mystique of the solitary romantic artist who could pretend to cosmic knowledge without the necessary university credentials was indeed welcome news, and without much regret the culture of Author-hood and Authority was shouldered aside. "Once the Author is removed, the claim to decipher a text becomes quite futile. . . . We know that to give writing its future, it is necessary to overthrow the myth: the birth of the reader must be at the cost of the death of the Author."[3]

Such was the Paris of 1968. Meanwhile, back in California, people couldn't care less about such remote issues of European thought. The electronic counterculture, and not literary high culture, was giving body to the *zeitgeist* and in an elitist diminuendo, first Aldous Huxley, then Alan Watts, then Timothy Leary, and then Jerry Garcia and The Grateful Dead worked to extend explorations with drugs to the new postindustrial masses who were about to find themselves in the new musical economy of the global village.

Intellectual fashions, much like those of *couture,* stimulate changes that are not so much developments as reactions and a mere craving that signals boredom and a desire to mark the new decade with a new style. So the liberationism of the 1960s led to the reactionary "New Age" movement of the 1970s, one in which the counterculture became caught up in the precivilized "epistemes" of megalithic stone circles, dowsing, witchcraft, palmistry, shamanism, and all the esoteric schools of the world religions that were not popular with clerical orthodoxy: namely, Kabbalah, Sufism, Zen, Tibetan Tantra, Yoga, and the Christian mystics from Meister Eckhart to Thomas Merton. This fashion, in turn, generated its reaction in the 1980s, as the populace swung back to fundamentalisms in Christianity and Islam, and capitalist neoconservatism in the governments of Thatcher, Reagan, and Kohl.

Just as the scholarly and introverted style of Aldous Huxley became vulgarized by Timothy Leary, so the New Age movement, initiated by the quiet introvert David Spangler in a remote village in Northern Scotland,[4] became vulgarized by

---

[3] Roland Barthes, "The Death of the Author" in *Image, Music, Text* (New York: Hill and Wang, 1977), p. 148.

[4] See David Spangler, *Revelation: The Birth of a New Age* (Findhorn, Scotland: 1971).

Shirley MacLaine in television specials and book dumps in su-
permarkets. These vulgarizations at once express the distribution of a message to its largest audience but also an addition of
noise picked up by the transmitting medium that overwhelms
the signal and indicates that the communication has become
more mess than message and has lost its integrity as it begins
to dissolve into cultural entropy. Ennui quickly follows excitement and people begin to look around for new signals to flash
their passage through time.

With the replacement of bookstores by supermarket
chains, the only books that are now available are books by
movie stars and TV celebrities. In a *differance,* the text is a sign
of being famous, and the famous are simply those who are
famous for being famous. An appearance on a TV show is
itself an achievement, an epiphany of the culture. A text in
this world is not meant to be read: it is simply another form of
currency and a means of exchange. In the consequent
breakup of culture into subcultures, intellectual respectability
must come from its unavailability and its resistance to communication and exchange, much like the heavy gold stored
under the *Paradeplatz* in Zürich, and so incomprehensibility
becomes the essential value. Here, the Europeans come back
into their own, and no American professors can hope to compete with the likes of Derrida and Habermas.

The end result of such a system of electronic communication and societal fragmentation is the return of the Middle
Ages. The bourgeois mass culture of industrial society breaks
up for good. The rich get richer, the poor get poorer and are,
as with the illegal Hispanic immigrants in the sun belt of the
United States, forced to become a servant class once again.
The draft and G.I. Joe are replaced by professional soldiers
and antiterrorist SWAT teams, and massive retaliation in thermonuclear war is replaced by smart weaponry in the hands of
cybernetic knights. Even in the civilian sector, new knights of
information begin to communicate through electronic mod-
ems mounted on personal computers. Publication is replaced

by "privacation" via electronic conferencing, and the bureau-cracies of universities begin to be challenged by hundreds of new and smaller tactical institutes of knowledge. The elec-tropeasantry follow the spectacles of the media, superstitiously believing in the power of their President or the patriotic vir-tues of Colonel North as once they believed in the power of their local patron saint, and the dwindling numbers of the in-telligentsia, shrinking from the thought that Shirley MacLaine and Phil Donahue have become the new American *philosophes* of the meaning of life, withdraw into the intellectual feudalism of their electronic cottages and chateaux.

From one point of view, all this furious media activity of action and reaction is like a child's teeter-totter fixed to a very flat ground. Everyone has a lot of fun and exercise, but the activitity goes nowhere. In a teeter-totter, what is exciting is the sensation of a sudden drop that is a celebration of a change of position, and so it is with these decadal shifts. It is the sudden shift from Marxism or drugs to the rigors of yogic discipline and diet, or from long hair and jeans to short hair and New Wave suits, or simply from yippie to yuppie, that is the essential experience being celebrated. It is the structure and not the content that is important, and any change will do as long as there is a generational consensus that this fashion captures the spirit of the decade.

As one gets older and bored with the teeter-totter, the mo-notony of the intensely spiked wavelength is no longer inter-esting and one gets off to allow the younger kids their turn in the playground. One joins the contemplative old people on the bench and begins to consider the longer wavelength, not simply of the passing decades of the 1960s, 1970s, and 1980s, but of whole civilizations. One begins to take in the entire field of playground, city, landscape, culture, and planet, and on, as far as one cares to take it in one's meditations on "the pattern that connects."

But not everything in nature is a question of connection and continuity, for the breaks, disruptions, discontinuities, and sudden shifts are equally important in the process of events. If what one is looking at is not simply the dripping of a faucet, or the passing of decades, but the passing of a world view, then any threshold that permits us to pass in and out of cosmologies provides us with an opportunity to understand how historical mentalities form and fall.

Of course, one cannot go back to the task of explication as if those Parisian 1960s had never taken place. As the 1960s themselves become ancient history for a generation of undergraduates that has no need of liberating itself from the oppressive weight of literacy, a glance backward can reveal that those elitist apostles of 1968, Barthes, Foucault, and Derrida, were indeed sensitive to the societal transformation of our time and that their writings, in fact, mark the change from a literate, European civilization to a global electronic culture. McLuhan may have been more popular, but certainly no one understood more quickly than Derrida the new world economy in which there was no absolute value, for currencies or commodities, but only an endless system of deferrals in the shifting arbitrage of currencies from New York to Tokyo to Hong Kong to Zürich to London to New York. As Derrida was pondering "The End of the Book and the Beginning of Writing,"[5] Nixon was deconstructing the text of the Bretton Woods global monetary system with its fixed values of exchange for the printed book of the American dollar; and as *differance* became the new source of wealth, electronics replaced paper. As the space of the marketplace expanded to a planetary scale, the time of the transaction contracted to seconds. Both the time and the space of the human event dissolved and the individual became an impulse in the global lattice. The space for perspective and the time for reflection, that whole mentality of Renaissance modernism that had

---

[5] See Jacques Derrida, "The End of the Book and the Beginning of Writing" in *Of Grammatology,* Trans. G. C. Spivak (Baltimore: Johns Hopkins University Press, 1974).

brought forth the individual in his or her booklined study, were transformed. For the young, reading could never again become the mystery school of individuation; printed laws, parliaments, and the territorial nation-state gave way to musical polities, and sound itself became the solvent of individuality: in rock concerts and discotheques the young played the music so loud that the flesh of the body vibrated, and a noetic ecosystem was brought forth out of noise.

One literary way to begin to understand this disorienting shift from one world structure to another is to reflect on previous modes of world construction. If we reflect our own condition in the antique mirror of Grimm, we can, perhaps, begin to see how a fairy tale can express a lost cosmology, and we can then begin to appreciate how the electronic folk arts of our own popular culture may be expressing a newly emergent property in the evolution of consciousness.

To experience a fairy tale, one must first hear it as speech, as a sound that connects, by hearth or bed, one human to another, and only after this participatory mode has been felt or imagined should one pass over to the culture of literacy to read it as a text on several levels at once. For this ontology of the text, it is not a question of a shifting system of *differance,* but coherence. We have to recover an intellectual sympathy for a culture in which both the Bible and the world were seen as texts of God. In that past culture of explication, as classically expressed in Dante's letter to Can Grande della Scala, a text had the archetypal structure of four levels of meaning: the *narrative,* the *allegorical,* the *moral,* and the *anagogical.* And I, too, shall wish to unfold my intellectual story on four levels of reading Grimms' fairy tale of "Rapunzel." The first level is the *literal* level of the story that the fairy tale narrates. The second level is the *structural* level in which we notice that there are *patterns* in the narration, but we do not rush to organize these patterns into an interpretive schema, be it Freudian or Marxian. The third level is the *anthropological* level in which we recognize that the narration is telling more than one story, that something else is going on in the description of psychological and sociological transformations. The fourth level is the *cosmological* level in which one realizes that the story is also about the setting up of an order that is not simply familial or societal, but planetary; that, in fact, the story is one of the setting up of a world system with its new relationships between the sexes, its new societal organization, and its new arrangement of the planets in the solar system. We do well, in the English language, to call these *Märchen* "fairy tales," for they are indeed expressions of a greatly expanded view of nature, one that is astonishingly supranatural.

2. THE LITERAL LEVEL

LET US, THEN, begin at the literal level, by hearing once again the narration of the story itself. The following is my own translation from the German of the Brothers Grimm, but to heighten the heard quality of the fairy tale as speech I have set the lines into a format of free verse in order to break up the block of textual prose and to isolate and heighten each narrative element as it comes forth from speech, touches the imagination, and associates the elements in the structures of emergent form.[6]

RAPUNZEL

Once there was a man and a woman,
who for so long a time wished in vain
to have a child;
but finally the woman became expectant
that the Dear Lord would fulfill her wish.

---

[6] *Kinder und Hausmärchen, Gesammelt Durch die Bruder Grimm,* I Band (Zürich: Manese Verlag, 1946), 102–107.

Now these people had at the back of their house
a little window through which one could see
a splendid garden that stood full
of the most beautiful flowers and herbs.
It was, however, surrounded by a high wall,
and no one dared to go in there,
because it belonged to a sorceress
who had great power and was feared in all the world.

Now one day the woman stood by this window
and looked down into the garden,
and there she saw a bed that was planted
with the most beautiful rapunzel,
and it seemed so fresh and green
that she began to feel the greatest longing and craving
to eat some of this rapunzel.
Well, the craving grew day by day,
until, as she knew she could not have any of it,
she began to waste away
and seemed so pale and miserable.

Then the husband became frightened and asked:
"What is it that you need, dear Wife?"
"Oh," she answered, "if I cannot get,
out of the garden behind our house,
any rapunzel to eat,
then I shall die."
Now the husband, who loved his wife so,
thought that before he would let his wife die,
he would fetch her some of the rapunzel,
cost what it may.

And so in the evening twilight
he climbed over the wall
down into the garden of the sorceress,
cut in a great hurry
a handful of rapunzel

and brought it to his wife.
Immediately she made herself a salad with it
and ate it all up with a hearty appetite.
But so good, so very good
did it taste to her,
that on the next day
she felt three times as much a craving for it.
If she were to have peace,
her husband yet once more
would have to climb down into the garden.

Once again in the evening twilight
he let himself down,
but this time as he clambered down the wall,
he shrank back suddenly
as he saw the sorceress standing before him.
"How can you dare,"
spoke she with an angry look,
"climb into my garden and like a thief
try to steal my rapunzel?
This is going to bring you harm."

"Oh," he answered, "let right give way to mercy,
for I only decided on this purpose out of need.
My wife saw your rapunzel out of the window,
and felt so great a craving that she would die
if she was not able to get any to eat."

Then the sorceress relented in her anger
and said to him, "Let it be as you say,
for I will permit you to take the rapunzel,
as much as you like,
only I make one condition:
you must give me the child
that your wife will bring into the world.
It shall go well with it
and I shall care for it like a mother."

In his fear the husband agreed to everything,
and as the wife came to childbed,
the sorceress immediately appeared,
gave the child the name of Rapunzel
and took it away with her.

Rapunzel was the most beautiful child under the sun.
As she became twelve years old,
the sorceress took her to the forest
and enclosed her in a tower,
which had neither door nor staircase,
but only high up a very little window.
When the sorceress wished to enter,
she placed herself there and cried:

"Rapunzel, Rapunzel,
Let down your hair."

Rapunzel had long, splendid hair,
fine as spun gold.
And when she heard the voice of the sorceress,
she untied her braids,
unwound them over the windowsill
and let her hair fall
twenty yards down below,
so that the sorceress could climb up.

After a few years it happened
that the son of the King was riding
through the forest and came past the tower.
There he heard a song that was so lovely,
that he held himself still and listened.
It was Rapunzel
who in her loneliness to while away the time
would let her sweet voice resound.
The King's son wanted to climb up to her
and sought for a door to the tower,
but there was none to find.

Rapunzel: Cosmology Lost

And so he rode home,
but the song had so stirred his heart
that he went out every day into the forest to listen.

Once as he was standing behind a tree,
he saw the sorceress come by
and heard how she cried out:

"Rapunzel, Rapunzel,
Let down your hair."

Then Rapunzel let down her long braids,
and the sorceress climbed up to her.
"Is that the ladder with which one comes up,"
said the King's son, "so once will I also try my luck."
And on the following day,
as it began to grow dark,
he went to the tower and cried:

"Rapunzel, Rapunzel,
Let down your hair."

Immediately the hair fell down,
and the King's son climbed up.

At first Rapunzel shrank back in fear,
as a man came toward her,
for she had never set eyes on a man before,
but when the King's son began
to speak to her in so completely a friendly manner
and to explain to her that it was her song
that had so moved his heart
that he could have no peace
unless he saw her himself,
then Rapunzel lost her fear.
And when he asked her
whether she would take him as a husband,
she saw how young and handsome he was,
and she thought: I would rather have him

15

than the old woman Gothel, and said yes
and lay her hand in his hand.
And so it was she said: "I will gladly go with you,
but I do not know how I can come down from here.
When you come, bring each time a strand of silk
with which I will braid a ladder,
and when it is ready,
then I will climb down
and you can take me away on your horse."

They arranged that he should come to her every evening,
for by day the old woman came.
But the sorceress noticed nothing about it all,
until once Rapunzel began to speak to her:
"Tell me, then, Frau Gothel, how does it happen
that you seem so much harder to draw up
than the young King's son
who will be with me in a moment."
"Oh, you godless child!" cried the sorceress,
"what must I hear from you.
I thought I had cut you off from all the world,
but you have betrayed me!"
In her anger she grabbed the beautiful hair of Rapunzel,
wound it twice around her left hand,
and, snip, snap, in an instant,
it was cut off and the beautiful braids
lay upon the earth.
And then she was so unmerciful
that she brought the poor Rapunzel into a wasteland,
where in great sorrow and wretchedness she had to live.

But on the very same day,
on which Rapunzel had been cast out,
at evening the sorceress fastened the braids
to the windowsill, and as the King's son came and cried:

"Rapunzel, Rapunzel,
Let down your hair."

It was she who let the hair fall down.
The King's son climbed up,
but above he did not find his beloved Rapunzel,
but the sorceress
who with evil and poisonous gaze glared at him.
"Aha!" she cried mockingly,
"you want to fetch your loving wife,
but the beautiful bird sits no more in the nest
and sings no more;
the cat has seized her
and now will also scratch out your eyes.
For you is Rapunzel lost,
you will never look at her again."
The King's son cried out in pain,
and in his desperation he jumped down from the tower.
He was able to save his life, but the thorns
into which he fell pricked his eyes.
Then he wandered blindly around in the forest,
ate nothing but roots and berries,
and did nothing but lament and cry
over the loss of his beloved wife.

And so he wandered about
for some years in misery
until at last he rode into the wasteland
where Rapunzel with the twins that she had given birth to,
a boy and a girl,
lived so wretchedly.
He heard a voice
and it seemed so familiar to him
that he went toward it,
and as he came closer,
Rapunzel recognized him
and fell about his neck and cried.
But two of her tears moistened his eyes,
so that they became clear again
and he could see with them as before.

And then he led her into his kingdom
where he was received with joy
and they lived long
and happily pleased everafter.

3. THE STRUCTURAL LEVEL

THE NARRATIVE LEVEL of the fairy tale unrolls the linear
sequence of events, but the structural level is the secondary
one in which one begins to notice *patterns* of images and
events. For the child, these patterns will be innocent and unconscious, and he or she may not be able to articulate why
such structures as the beauty and the beast, or the witch and
the child, are so fascinating; the child will only be able to respond with wide eyes and an intensity of attention that marks
the power or the patterning of imagery to catch hold of the
imagination. One can notice this difference in intensity when
one compares the narrative power of Grimms' fairy tales to
stories that are too rationalized, contrived, and adult. Stories
such as Antoine de Saint Exupery's *Le petit prince* or Michael
Ende's *Momo* are conceived by and for adults with what Jung
would call a *Puer eternus* complex, but the fairy tales that the
Brothers Grimm collected come out of the darkness of lost
time with a primordial power that holds children and adults in
complete absorption.

For the adult who tells or reads the story, the patterns will
begin to register and the narrative line of the story will begin
to generate another line of reflection. At first, this other line
will be simply one of an awareness of parallelism and sim-
ilarities, then, perhaps, a clustering of images that will enhance the imaginative intensity of the pictures in one's mind.
As one begins to think about this reflected line and to com-
pare the second line to the first, then one begins to wonder
and consider possible meanings these images could have.
When patterns begin to connect to other patterns, they lead to

discoveries. It is a simple matter of the search: "If this is here, then perhaps that is over there." And as we dig in a new place we find much more than we expected. But at first, it is simply a matter of little details and not large discoveries; one notices that there is a little window in the house, *ein kleines Fenster* and a little window in the tower, *ein kleines Fensterchen*. One notices that the garden is surrounded by a wall and that the tower is surrounded by thorn bushes. And one notices that the men in the story must climb up, but as they come down, they get into trouble with the sorceress. The husband must climb up the wall, and the Prince must climb up the tower, but when they descend, they both find themselves under the power of the sorceress. Here one notices that this sorceress is a creature of significant powers, for she is never described as simply a *böse Hexe* or evil witch, but always with the more important title of *Zauberin*. This makes her a person of knowledge and not simply an old hag with evil intentions.

As one begins to think about these little details, one observes that the story has a good deal to say about food: the food in the garden, the salad of rapunzel, and the food in the wasteland, the roots and berries of the gatherer and not the food of the more settled gardener. The pattern seems to repeat itself with a fondness for twos and the story unfolds a whole series of sets and pairs: a man and a woman, then the old woman and the maiden, then the adolescent woman and the prince, then the twins, the boy and the girl to whom Rapunzel gives birth.

4. THE ANTHROPOLOGICAL LEVEL

SCHOLARS OF MYTH as different as Mircea Eliade and Claude Lévy-Strauss have demonstrated, in their studies of androgynes and incest, that the problem of how "the one becomes two" is a central concern to the mythopoeic mentality. Stories as different as that of Adam and Eve in the Near East or of Asdiwal in the Pacific Northwest are attempts to resolve the contradictions and tensions that seem to be inherent in sexuality. Since Rapunzel gives birth to twins, one begins to suspect that this fairy tale is also an attempt to show "how the one becomes two."

As the sets of pairs begin to come and go in the story, we notice that some couples are unstable and have difficulty holding their endurance through time, and that others are more stable; that indeed one of the themes of the story is the achievement of a stable couple. The husband and the wife at the beginning of the story do not seem to be a stable couple, and the wife's craving takes her back to a longing for the food that is in the sorceress's garden. Her pregnancy craving points up the inadequacy of the powers of the husband and he becomes reduced to the role of a hopeless go-between with one woman full of the power of childbirth on the inside and another full of the wisdom of plants on the outside. The little window at the back of the house seems to be looking back to the past and the unstable husband begins to behave not so much like a father in a stable patriarchy, but a mother's brother in a matriarchy. As with the case of St. Joseph and Mary in pregnancy, where the child does not really belong to him, one begins to suspect that the child really belongs to the society of women. As in the case of "The Cherrytree Carol" in which Mary's pregnancy craving is for a fruit, the mysteries of childbirth take us back into another and more ancient system of knowledge that has to do with plants and women. Pregnancy itself sets up a craving for the old order at the back of time, the order of women's mysteries, the neolithic order of gardening, midwifery, and the medicinal lore of plants.[7] The wife in her time needs what the old woman has in abundance.

---

[7] For a much lengthier discussion of midwifery and cosmology, see W. I. Thompson, *The Time Falling Bodies Take to Light: Mythology, Sexuality, and the Origins of Culture,* Chapter Two, "Symbolization" (New York: St. Martin's Press, 1981).

The old woman is not a witch, but a sorceress and as such she is a woman of knowledge, of the lore of plants and cosmologies that have to do with the moon and women's mysteries of menstruation and childbirth. The only characters who bear proper names in the tale are Frau Gothel and Rapunzel. Gothel means Bright God and Rapunzel means rampion in English, and the fact that the woman and the girl are so highlighted with names suggests that this couple represents a relationship to the old world of lunar cosmology and the lore of plants. The archaic, prehistoric couple is not the husband and the wife, but the old woman and the maiden. This couple is the ancient one of Demeter and Persephone, or the even older, neolithic couple, the woman and the maiden that was sculpted on the walls of Catal Hüyük in prehistoric Anatolia.

This most ancient pair lasts for a long time and represents a more stable coupling than the man and the wife, or the Prince and Rapunzel in the tower. Men are interlopers, and the reason that the husband so easily assents to the sorceress's demands is that in the religion of women's mysteries, she is the Midwife, and the child belongs to her and to her body of knowledge.

But there is a new magic to Rapunzel, for she does not simply give birth to another child to continue the line in a simple progression down through unchanging time; she gives birth to twins, and in myth the birth of twins is always a numinous event. Somehow Rapunzel has it in her to resolve the central problem, for she is the one that can produce two, and not simply two daughters in the mother-daughter cloning of parthogenesis, but the mother that can produce a boy and a girl. The story begins "There was once a man and a woman," and ends with a boy and a girl and a man and a woman who are able to live happily ever after in the kingdom of the father and the grandfather. We begin the story with a weak and unstable patrilocal society bordering on the neolithic garden of the ancient matriarchy, but we end the story with the achievement of a stable patriarchy in the realm of the King. Civilization has been achieved, and the tragically volatile and dangerous power of sexuality has been sublimated into a higher form, not of a village bordering on a garden, but a real civilization with a king.

The process of sublimation, or of raising up, is clearly one of the other patterns that one notices in the story. The husband must climb up the wall that separates his home from the sorceress's and then descend into the garden and power of the old woman. The Prince must climb the tower, and then fall into the deadlier plants that blind him and cast him out from his father's kingdom into the wasteland, where he regresses to the most ancient past of gathering. The German version of the story does not say why the Prince was in the forest in the first place; it would be neat and symmetrical if he went there to hunt, for then the hunting of men would be contrasted to the gardening and gathering of women.[8] But blinded by the thorns of the old hag, he is not able to exercise manly power and control to hunt in the forest and the wasteland; he is reduced to a woman's diet of roots and berries. Man, the hunter, moves farther back in time to the most ancient food of all as he becomes a blind and primitive gatherer.

But as there is indeed a magic to Rapunzel, the tears that come out of her are able to cure the male's blindness. Here one notices a pattern of "as above, so below," for the male fluid that comes out of the testicles at the bottom of the spinal column is able to make Rapunzel pregnant, but the female fluid that comes out of the eyes at the top of the spinal column is able to cure male blindness. R. B. Onians has excavated the prehistoric European physiology in which the semen and the cerebral fluid were thought to be in communication through the spinal column; one carried one's seed in one's head, and

---

[8] The French version of the tale, which is much more focused on food and its elimination, does make the contrast between male hunting and female gathering quite explicit. *"Un jour, le fils du roi, étant à la chasse, a l'occasion de voir comment la belle jeune fille monte lafée."* See Paul Delarue, *Le Conte populair français* (Paris: Éditions Erasme, 1957), p. 176.

all the bodily fluids were full of magical power.[9] This ancient Indo-European lore was rendered into an explicit philosophy of sexuality and transformation in Tantra Yoga, a philosophy and practice in which semen is seen to have numinal powers not restricted to sexual reproduction. The tears of Rapunzel that come from her heart of love and compassion seem to produce a "higher knowledge" in which she can serve as a more loving example of women's knowledge, a figure of the Sophia archetype. When this higher fluid is added by the female to the lower generative fluid of the male, or as Goethe would poetically express it, when *"Das Ewig-Weibliche Zieht uns hinan,"* then a truly stable couple of male and female is achieved and they are able to live, no longer under the power of the old lunar hag, but in the more extensive realm of the solar King.

That "Rapunzel" is not simply a story about sexuality, but *the story* of sexuality is immediately apparent in the opening lines: *"Es war einmal ein Mann und eine Frau . . ."* Indeed, the whole fairy tale can be seen as an exploration of the comparative stability of the mother-daughter pair versus the husband and wife pair, an exploration, that in the *mythologique* that Lévy-Strauss has described, is a narrative that is trying to resolve the contradiction of the one and the two, as well as the contradictory nature of sexuality itself. In fact, the more one knows about the nature and cultural history of sexuality, the richer this little fairy tale becomes.

So, let us consider the *nature* of sexuality for a moment. "Rapunzel" is a story named after a particular plant, and it was with the most primitive plants, the blue-green algae, or what are now called cyanobacteria, that our atmospheric world first evolved. As the microbiologists Panisset and Sonea have pointed out:

---

[9] See R. B. Onians, *The Origins of European Thought About the Body, the Mind, the Soul, the World, Time, and Fate* (Cambridge, England: Cambridge University Press, 1951), p. 109. See also Norman O. Brown, *Love's Body* (New York: Vintage, 1968), p. 136.

Cyanobacteria live at the surface of bodies and release free oxygen as a result of their type of photosynthesis. Their ancestors are most likely to have been responsible for the first appearance of oxygen in the terrestrial atmosphere, leading later to the advent of aerobic bacteria, and, much later, to the appearance of eukaryotes.[10]

Commenting upon the work of her colleagues Panisset and Sonea and developing the theory of the evolution of sexuality, the microbiologist Lynn Margulis has noted that:

If vagaries of environment did not exist, and if weather, climate and geological phenomena were predictable and regular, then sex might never have evolved. In fact, certain highly successful organisms, such as sponges and a huge group of fungi (the fungi imperfecti), living in stable environments, have reverted to asexuality, and produce offspring like their parent. Over most of the world, however, change is the rule and species with the capacity for sexual reproduction of offspring are more plastic, more versatile than those that receive all their genes from a single parent.
. . . Some two billion years ago, cynobacteria made drastic changes in the atmosphere. It is doubtful that any organisms since have had such a profound effect on the planet.[11]

In the evolution of sexuality the critical event is that of the emergence of the cell with a nucelus, the eukaryotic cell. Hitherto, nature had worked through an asexual division ad infinitum of mother-daughter cells in which each generation was exactly like the preceding one. The cell without a nucleus, the prokaryotic cell, was a stable, unchanging, and enduring system, but the cell with a nucleus introduces the radically destabilizing element of the individual. But with the emergence of the individual falls the shadow of the old hag of death. The

---

[10] Sorin Sonea and Maurice Panisset, *A New Bacteriology* (Boston: Jones & Bartlett, 1983), p. 60.

[11] Lynn Margulis, *Early Life* (Boston: Jones & Bartlett, 1984), pp. 126, 138. See also Lynn Margulis and Dorion Sagan, *The Origins of Sex: Three Billion Years of Genetic Recombination* (New Haven: Yale University Press, 1986).

price of sexuality and individuation is death. Eros and Thanatos, long before Freud put forth his interpretation, were inseparably linked in the cultural history of myth and the natural history of the evolution of life.

The appearance of sexuality is, therefore, a disruption of the stable and enduring system of mother-daughter replication. And in the natural war of replication versus reproduction, the male is the intruder, the interloper, the disrupter of the ancient order. He rides forth to steal Persephone away from Demeter. Notice once again how women are associated with plants in mythology, for Persephone is associated with the Asphodel, just as Rapunzel is associated with Rampion; but notice also how these two stories are reversed mirror images, for in one the maiden picks the plant and is seized by the male, and in the other the man picks the plant and is seized by the woman. Whether we are considering Demeter and her search for her stolen daughter or the lament of the Queen of the Night in Mozart's *The Magic Flute,* what we are seeing expressed in the myth, the fairy tale, and the work of art is the tragic story of the evolution of life, the story of love and death. In Mozart's aria, the Queen of the Night is not simply resounding with the cry of the prehistoric matriarchy against the cruelties of the civilized patriarchy, she is giving voice to all life and the cry of the prokaryotic cell against the new order of the eukaryotic cell. Such is the power of myth, and such is the imaginative power of art.

With the appearance of death, time takes on a new triangular shape of sprouting, flowering, and withering. Robert Graves has traced this "Triple Goddess" all the way back to megalithic Newgrange,[12] so the fact that there are Three Ladies in *The Magic Flute,* and three women in *Rapunzel,* should alert us to this most ancient threefold pattern of the maiden, the pregnant woman, and the old crone. These three women, in turn, are matched by the three men of the King,

[12] Robert Graves, *The White Goddess* (New York: Farrar Straus & Giroux, 1975).

the King's son, and the husband who is, in actuality, the mother's brother of the older matrilineal order. And, for the greater part of the story, it is precisely this matrilineal order that is the stronger. Neither the husband nor the Prince is equal to the power of the sorceress. Through the power of fear the husband shrinks back at the sight of the sorceress, and the Prince jumps back at the sight of the old hag and falls into the thorns.

Regression is one of the major themes of this fairy tale, for when the Prince wanders in the wasteland and is reduced to eating roots and berries, he is regressing from civilization to savagery; but there is also an earlier regression that is being dramatized here, just as there is in the aria of the Queen of the Night. In many fairy tales the witch or the dwarf, as is the case in the equally famous tale of *Rumpelstilzchen,* demands the firstborn child as the price of cooperation. The jealousy of the dwarves and "the little people" is an essential part of the animistic religion of the fairy faith, and when one realizes that these "little people" are mythopoeic perceptions of what we prefer to call bacteria, then one realizes that these "elementals" are indeed the "firstborn" creatures on this planet, and that we eukaryotic creatures of individuality, of love and death, have displaced them. In Jesus's parable of the vineyard, they are the workers of the first hour who resent that the first have become last. Displaced from their position of primacy, the elementals seek revenge upon the children of humanity and demand that their firstborn be sacrificed, just as they were.

The archetypal narrative power of the sorceress comes from her ability as an image to recapitulate many levels of order in the vastness of time. She is the midwife, which in French is more appropriately called *la sage femme* and as such she represents the knowledge of the old lunar cosmology. As an archaic figure of lost time, however, she also becomes a symbol of the vast reaches of time, not simply the matrilineal order that stood for millennia before the recent patrilineal order, but also the prokaryotic order that stood for a billion years before the eukaryotic. In seizing the child, the sorceress is at once regressing back from patriarchy to matriarchy, and from sexual reproduction to asexual replication. The wall that surrounds the husband's house was to keep her out, but in transgressing it, he has released the primordial powers of the past to overwhelm and swamp the present generation.

When the mother looks out the window at the back of the house, she is looking to the past and unconsciously summoning *la sage femme* who can help her in her labor. But the past is connected to a deeper past, and the sorceress is the embodiment of the lore of plants and the roots of knowledge that go all the way back to women's transformation of gathering into gardening in the neolithic era. But even this past is connected to a still-deeper past that is concerned with the evolution of plants themselves. Before there were males and females and

Figure 1. *Cyanobacterium (Aphanothece). (Photo: John F. Stolz)*

sexual reproduction, there was asexual replication. The earliest plants in the evolution of life, those that first introduced the process of photosynthesis were the cyanobacteria. The woman in her craving looks back through the window to the past and sees the beautiful walled garden with all its neat rows of the beds of rapunzel, and these beds themselves harken back to the first geometry of photosynthesis, for a cyanobacterium has its internal photosynthesizers on membranes alligned in rows. Indeed, the photograph of a cyanobacterium in Figure 1 looks very much like an aerial photograph of a walled garden with its neat beds of plants. Through turning on an evolutionary spiral in which one image is a recapitulation of an earlier image, we begin to behold an image cluster, and, perhaps, this can provide us with a functional definition of "an archetypal image." We intuit what we do not know, and one may say that the imagination is just this capacity to feel and experience elements beyond our more limited and personal range of ratiocinative knowledge. A woman in pregnancy is a creature filled with unconscious cravings that men think funny, but in the old knowledge of the lost cosmology, these cravings are surfacings of real needs in understanding the medicinal power of plants. The mother could not rest content in the house of the male; in feeling the pregnancy engendered in her by the intrusion of the male and his seed, she looked out the little window to the past and longed for the old food of the good old days of neolithic gardening in a time before there were such things as husbands and fathers.

I have used the term "anthropological" rather than sociological to explicate this level of the narrative because I wish to indicate the unity of the external sociological dimension with the internal, psychological one. In the lunar cosmology of the past, the inside and the outside are in an intimate participation whose sign is the moon, for the lunar mysteries are precisely those in which the most internal movements of menstruation are in harmony with the movements of the external heavenly bodies. It is only for us moderns that the psychological dimension is felt to be merely subjective and epi-phenomenal to the hard, objective realities of war and business and science. But in the archaic mentality that this fairy tale so beautifully unfolds, the psychological dimension is inseparable from the social; consequently, the story is not sim-ply one of regression from patrilineal to matrilineal culture but a progression to a new level of individuation and wisdom.

A Jungian analysis of the tale, in the hands of an Erich Neumann or a Marie-Louise von Franz,[13] would recognize the shift in the sociological order, but they would both see a story of the movement away from the feminine as the all-encom-passing and imprisoning "dragon mother" to the higher femi-nine, the "Sophia" of Rapunzel, not as maiden, but as mother of twins. The Prince at the beginning of the story is the ele-mentary male, one who hears Rapunzel's call, overcomes the barrier, and immediately seeks to mate with her. The male, under the dominance of his instincts, will say anything to achieve copulation. The female's response is to work to chan-nel this drive into nest building, and so Rapunzel sets the Prince to work to braid her a ladder with which she can safely escape the power of the old crone. Because all the psychic en-ergy of the male is focused at the level of the genitals, his domination by instinct brings him face to face with the domin-ion of the dragon-mother of a nature that is blind when ruled only by instinct and passion. And so the Prince falls into the thorns that surround the tower, regresses to the savagery that stood before civilization, and wanders blind in the wilderness. After a period of purgation, suffering, and loneliness, he has become purified of the dominance of his instincts, hears again the song of Rapunzel, but this time he is not driven simply by an instinctive drive, but rather one of longing and love. In their conjunction here, it is the "higher" female fluid of the

---

[13] See Erich Neumann, *The Great Mother* (Princeton, N.J.: Princeton University Press, 1972), and Marie-Louise von Franz, *Shadow and Evil in Fairy Tales* (Zürich: Springer Verlag, 1974).

eyes, the organ of sight and understanding, that cures his male blindness of instinctive drives. Rapunzel, at the end of the story, is no longer the ignorant maiden, bragging to her dragon-mother about her boyfriend, Prince Charming, who is about to visit her. She has become the wise woman who is able to resolve in her very center, in her womb, the central problem of "how the one can become two," for she is not only able to produce a daughter, after the archaic pattern of mother-daughter replication ad infinitum, she is able to produce a son. When the female can produce a male, the contradiction is resolved, and we have moved up to the "higher" level of sexual reproduction, the level of a stable couple, and a stable social order—not that of the weaker, half-individuated servant of the mother's brother, but the new order of sons, husbands, and fathers. And so it is that the King's son with his knowledge of the larger world is able to lead her out of the wilderness and into the vast realm of the King. The fairy tale thus unfolds the story of the formation of the psyche: the movement from eros to agapé, from the darkness of blind instinct to the tears of the higher feminine that bring illumination. In the genius of the fairy tale, the biological story of the evolution of life and the natural history of sexuality, as well as the sociological story of the evolution of individuality and wisdom, are all unrolled at once. That would be enough for any great story, but that is not the end of this extraordinary story, for there is still another level implicit in the narration, one that concerns not simply the formation of life, the formation of society, and the formation of the psyche, but the formation of the solar system and the setting up of a "world."

5. THE COSMOLOGICAL LEVEL

A PLANT THAT COULD stir up such longing is obviously no ordinary weed, and if the wisdom of the sorceress is based on the lore of plants, it is clear that one needs to take a closer look at this rapunzel on which the whole fairy tale is based.

And here is where the noticing of patterns begins to take one into other patterns, even before one has formulated an intellectual interpretation. As one pulls gently on the plant, the roots pull up a more deeply buried artifact of a lost world. When I asked myself: "Why is this particular plant chosen for the story?" I was not prepared for all the delightful surprises that were hidden in the earth still clinging to the roots of this story.

Rapunzel, or rampion, is *Campanula rapunculus;* it is a biennial herb that can be planted in the fall and harvested in the winter, and so it is very popular for use in winter salads. Both the roots and the leaves are edible, and its very tiny flower is pale blue, or a washed-out lilac color. But what is most interesting about this plant is that it is autogamous, or, as is the case with many flowers, hermaphroditic and endowed with the capacity to fertilize itself. A tall stem or column rises up and tries to attract insects to bring it the pollen from other plants, but if no pollination occurs, the column will split in two (the one becomes two again) and the halves will curl like braids or coils on a maiden's head, and this will bring the female stigmatic tissue into contact with the male pollen on the exterior surface of the stylar column. To help in the process of gathering the male pollen to itself, the column is endowed with "collecting hairs." (See Figure 2.) So rapunzel does indeed have a tower, does indeed send out a call for the male to come and pollinate her, and does indeed have "collecting hairs" that allow her to draw up the male into intimate contact with her reproductive organs. Many flowers have this hermaphroditic capacity of autogamy, or self-replication, but since the evolutionary emergence of sexuality, nature prefers to avoid "selfing," for selfing leads to inbreeding, loss of diversity, and loss of the adaptive flexibility to survive in changing circumstances. Often the male and female parts of a plant will mature at different times so that preference is given to attracting the pollen from other plants, rather than folding back onto itself in singular, if still genetically diploid, sexual reproduction. Sexuality, with its mixing of genes, allows for maximum adaptive

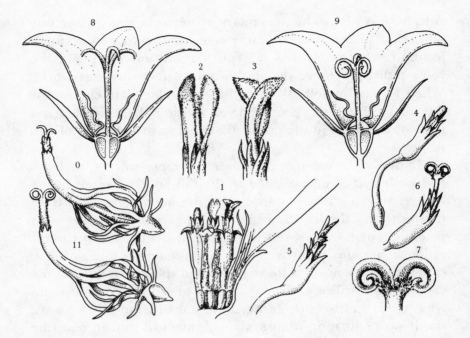

Figure 2. The stylar column of Campanula rapunculus.

flexibility, diversity, and the emergence of novelty. The one becomes two, and then that one becomes two again, ad infinitum. Appropriately enough for the life of this storied herb, the first sprout that appears from the planted seed splits into the neat bilateral symmetry of two leaves.

This fairy tale, obviously, emerges out of a culture with a deep knowledge of the life of plants; it would seem that the story itself is part of "the lore of plants" of *la sage femme,* for in some of the other European variants of this folk tale the association of the sorceress with plants is made even more magical, as she is termed a "Fee" or fairy.[14] In some of these variants, it is the mother herself who fetches the plant, and in the Italian and French versions the plant is parsley and not rapunzel. A craving for parsley of the mother would make immediate

[14] See Johannes Bolte und Georg Polivka, *Anmerkungen zu den Kinder und Hausmärchen der Brüder Grimm* (Leipzig: Dieterichische Verlag, 1913), pp. 97–99.

sense, for in European folk and herbal medicine, parsley is recommended as a cure for kidney and urinary problems, and such problems are not uncommon in pregnancy. In fact, the folk term for cystitis is "bride's disease," and the term reflects the sense that the intrusion of the male organ into the private parts of the female brings infection and discomfort as well as new life. The female in pregnancy is filled with the problem of how to contain this new way of life as the child presses down on her bladder, and how to eliminate the excess of life brought to her by the male. But if she seeks to regress to the prehistoric condition of the mother-daughter process of replication, she finds herself with yet another problem of space as she becomes the captive of the sorceress.

The significance of the plant rapunzel is more esoteric and less earthy. Fairy tales and folklore are always subject to a *bricolage* in which the teller of the tale adapts the story to local conditions, so this shift from parsley to rapunzel is not unusual. Like a kaleidoscope in which the patterns change with each shift, thus producing an individual meaning to each particular pattern, there still remains a consistent symmetry to the overall pattern of the folktale and its variants. Stories, as I have remarked before, are themselves a form of cultural storage, for knowledge will survive the transmission through images for many more generations than it ever could through mere conceptual duplication. Any teacher knows that it is difficult to have knowledge last even to the final exam, but a myth, a legend, or a fairy tale has the capacity to survive with its archetypal pattern intact for millennia. If I tell you that the earth's magnetic field deflects the proton bombardment of the solar wind, you will probably forget everything but the image of "the wind," and this will stick with you and transform into some fabled form. But if I say: "Father Sun shoot'em arrows at Mother Earth, but Mother Earth holds up big shield and knocks arrows away," you will get the whole pattern and be able to reproduce the story for generations. Even later, when the knowledge has been lost, the story will survive. When the male, patrilineal society of warriors lost all interest in and sensitivity for the ancient cosmology, the wise sorceress with her botanical and astrological knowledge became caricatured as an evil old witch with a foul-smelling cauldron of toads and weeds, but even in the society of warriors, the stories the nursemaid would tell would keep the narrative structure intact as the material made its way from myth to legend to oral fairy tale and on into Romanticism and the high arts of a literate, industrial civilization. As Robert Darnton has pointed out in his own journey into folklore:

> Folklorists have recognized their tales in Herodotus and Homer, on ancient Egyptian papyruses and Chaldean stone tablets; and they have recorded them all over the world, in Scandinavia, and Africa, among Indians on the banks of the Bengal and Indians along the Missouri. The description is so striking that some have come to believe in Ur-stories and a basic Indo-European repertory of myths, legends, and tales.[15]

When I first began to look at botanical text books to find out more about this herb, *Campanula rapunculus,* I had a hunch that the herb, like parsley, would be a medicinal one recommended for "women's complaints" or be of particular benefit in preventing miscarriage; but I had no idea that the sexual life of the plant would itself recapitulate the sexual drama of the fairy tale. I found no indication that the herb was prescribed by midwives, but I began to suspect that if my first recognition of one pattern connected to a hidden pattern, then there might be more yet to discover. The textbooks indicated that the flower of rapunzel was fivefold, and then I recognized the next level of "the pattern that connects."

Fivefold flowers are associated with the planet Venus. Indeed, one of them is even called "Venus's Looking Glass," and this is because the flower is a mirroring reflection of the pattern that the apparent movement of Venus makes in the sky. "As above, so below." That is to say, the apparent movement of the planet in the pre-Copernican world view, for in all this

---

[15] Robert Darnton, "Peasants Tell Tales" in *The Great Cat Massacre and Other Episodes in French Cultural History* (New York: Vintage, 1985), p. 21.

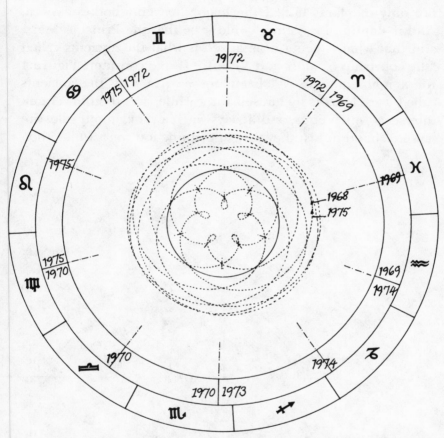

Figure 3. *The apparent motion of Venus.* (Drawing: Keith Critchlow)

ancient lore, we have indeed moved back in time before modern Renaissance astronomy. Figure 3 shows the pattern that Venus makes in the sky.[16]

If Rapunzel is Venus, then Frau Gothel, the "Bright God,"

---

[16] These charts are the work of the cultural historian Keith Critchlow and are taken from material presented by the Anthroposophical Society in Dornach, Switzerland. For a most important discussion of this ancient cosmology, see Keith Critchlow's "The Planets as Time Keepers: Patterns in Space and Time" in his book, *Time Stands Still: New Light on Megalithic Science* (New York: St. Martin's Press, 1980), pp. 150–168.

must be the moon, and the conjunction of the two is a story, not only of plants but of the major heavenly bodies as well. And if Rapunzel is Venus, could it be that the Prince is Mars, and that what is being dramatized is what the ancients called "the courtship of Mars and Venus"? If one considers Figure 4 for a moment, one will begin to see just why the ancients called it so. Mars is by himself for a while, and then his circuit intersects with Venus, and he lays with her, or, in our tale, she lays her hand in his; they stay in conjunction for a while, then

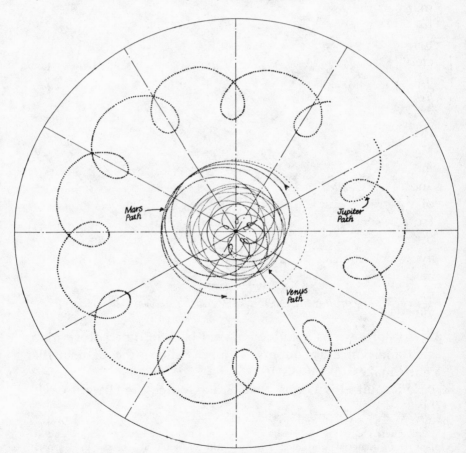

Figure 4. *The pattern of conjunction of Venus and Mars. (After Keith Critchlow)*

the moon returns, he is driven out and wanders into the wilderness, or the vast dark regions of the solar system, away from her and Earth. What Figure 4 shows, then, is the courtship of Mars and Venus, and it tells us once again that for the mythopoeic imagination of the ancients, knowledge, and complex astronomical knowledge, was stored in images and hieroglyphs. We moderns, with our prosaic, ratiocinative, reductionistically inclined minds that are addicted to statistics and linear quantification but not to pattern recognition, took many of these images literally in a stupid fundamentalist way, for this enabled us to debunk "the primitive, prescientific mentality" and feel confident in the triumphs of industrial society. But this is as stupid as someone in a future culture making fun of us because we spoke of solar *winds* and magnetic *fields,* as if space were some sort of park.

If Rapunzel is Venus, Frau Gothel the Moon, and the Prince Mars, then one suspects that the mother must be Mother Earth, and that the intimate relationship between the mother and the sorceress is the close relationship of the Earth and the Moon. Who then is the husband? If my interpretation of the tale is valid, and that the story is about the movement from an unstable couple to a stable couple in the achievement of a true husband and father, then the first husband is the avuncular mother's brother and not the father; since the husband plays the role of the messenger who goes back and forth to bring the mother what she needs, I suspect that he is Mercury, "the messenger of the gods." Mercury is called the messenger because it is a busy little planet, one that moves constantly back and forth, for in its circuit around the Earth, the pattern is not one of five, but twenty-two. (See Figure 5.) The King is, obviously, the Sun, and the vast reaches of his kingdom are the solar system itself. When Mars wanders out alone in the dark reaches of space, he is lost in the wilderness, but when he returns into conjunction with Venus, the family of planets is constellated. Similarly, when Venus rises out of the underworld as the morning star with the twin stars of Cas-

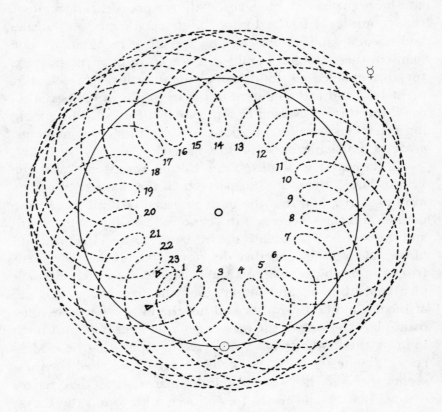

Figure 5. The apparent motion of Mercury. *(After Keith Critchlow)*

tor and Pollux in the sign of Gemini, which occurs in the springtime, she becomes the sign of the return of life and the coming abundance of the riches of the solar king, the summer's harvest and the continuity of life after the wasteland and suffering of winter. Quite interestingly, the conjunction of Venus with the twin stars in the sign of Gemini would occur in the period of 6000 to 4000 B.C., and this period, from Çatal Hüyük to the threshold of civilization in Mesopotamia, is indeed the climactic period of neolithic, matrilineal society. The iconography on the walls of Çatal Hüyük is that of the mother and the maiden, the twin goddess, but also found at the site were statues of the old crone, associated with vultures. The young male statues are buried in the vulture shrine in which the claws of the birds are depicted, so one can infer, because of the burial patterns of excarnation by birds that James Mellaart discusses, that here it is not the witch's cat that scratches out the Prince's eyes with thorns, but the vultures of the crone that tear out the eyes of the male. This is how the narrative structure, or archetype, can shift from one content to another but still keep the same form, just as a melody can modulate from one key to another but still keep the same melodic structure.

What our fairy tale is describing is the landscape of a lost world, the cosmology of what Marija Gimbutas calls "Old Europe,"[17] in the period around 4000 B.C. when the shift to patrilineal society is being felt, with all its tensions with the old ways of 6000 B.C. The fairy tale is itself a narrative of the transition from one Platonic "Magnus Annus," or zodiacal sign in the precession of the poles,[18] to another and is filled with a meticulous knowledge of botany and astrology and helps us to appreciate "the science of the concrete" of the prehistoric sorceress.

---

[17] See Marija Gimbutas, *The Gods and Goddesses of Old Europe: 7000–3500 B.C.* (London: Thames & Hudson, 1974).

[18] See Hertha von Dechend and Giorgio de Santillana, *Hamlet's Mill: An Essay on Myth and the Frame of Time* (Boston: Gambit, 1969).

It is curious that the German version of this fairy tale is so much more mystical and cosmological than the French version, for the processes of eating and elimination seem to be much more the focus of attention in the French variants in which the craving is for the diuretic herb parsley and in which the Prince and Persinette sew up the anus of the parrot that always betrays them to the fairy. What seems so pronounced in the German version is precisely the astronomical as opposed to the gastronomical, but then, considering the fundamental relationship of cuisine to culture in France, it is perhaps not all that surprising. In comparing the French variants to the German fairy tales collected by the Brothers Grimm, Robert Darnton has noted: "Where the French tales tend to be realistic, earthy, bawdy, and comical, the German veer off toward the supernatural, the poetic, the exotic, and the violent."[19]

Grimms' "Rapunzel" is indeed supernatural and poetic, but it is precisely because these poetic dimensions of the Imagination are present that a world can be brought forth that is so deep in its Indo-European roots and so rich in its cosmological complexity. The setting up of a stable world is set forth in a narrative of several levels: the bass line dramatizes the formation of a stable solar-system; the tenor line describes the formation of a stable, patrilineal society; the alto line describes the formation of a stable family; and the soprano line describes the formation of a stable psyche in the achievement of the illumination of the *Sophia* of the higher feminine. The old religion must now survive as an esoteric mystery school in the new exoteric society of princes and warriors. The very act of the narration of the story becomes an unconscious performance through art of this *Sophia* that speaks to the child and the artist who is willing to take time for such foolish things as fairy tales.

---

[19] Darnton, op. cit., p. 50.

In the more romantic era of the nineteenth century, the presence of such a complex cosmology would be interpreted to mean that the story had to have an author or authoress who could compose the story to sneak lost knowledge into a society that was turning away from the old religion. But now in the twentieth century with our new appreciation of "attractors" in the emergence of complex topologies, we do not need to be that simplistic to insist that an authorial person is required for the existence of such a cultural story. Scientists such as Manfred Eigen and Francisco Varela have shown how "autopoiesis" can emerge at the molecular and cellular levels,[20] so now we can begin to appreciate that nature has such marvelous complexities of immanental mind as "the organization of the living"[21] that form can emerge without "conscious purpose." Indeed, fairy tales are a very good place to notice the difference between the autopoietic "mind" of a naturally and culturally complex system and the more artificial intelligence of a mentally and consciously controlled narration by a modern artist who would try to write a fairy tale. So I would not wish my exercise in an archaeology of the unconscious interpreted in a literal, fundamentalist, "New Age" way to say that far back in 4000 B.C. a sorceress composed this story, or that in the eighteenth century Friedrich Schulz, one of the sources for the Brothers Grimm,[22] psychically channeled this neolithic story. What seems to me to be all the more marvelous and full of wonder is the "autopoiesis" of culture as a form of immanental mind that can remember more than it individually knows. Perhaps Roland Barthes was right after all, and in his all too French paricide of the Author is the end of the patriarchate of the French Academy, the end of literature as pri-

---

[20] See Erich Jantsch, *The Self-Organizing Universe* (Oxford: Pergamon Press, 1980).

[21] See Humberto Maturana and Francisco Varela, "Autopoiesis: The Organization of the Living" in *Autopoiesis and Cognition* (Boston: Reidel, 1980).

[22] Friedrich Schulz, *Kleinen Romanen* 5 (Leipzig, 1790), pp. 269–288.

41

vate property, and the return of *sorcellerie,* enchantment, and the community of life. As the forests die in Europe from the exhausts of male knights speeding in their big trucks and fast German cars, there is a turn of the spiral in which the old mystery school of plants is understood in the passing of one world into another. As one culture lived at the edge of a vanishing world in 4000 B.C., so do we now in 2000 A.D. Driving down the autobahn and looking around at the industrialized landscape, one knows that, whether from Greenhouse Effect or Ozone Hole, this world cannot last. In fact one becomes fascinated with narrations of world formation precisely because our world is coming apart. And when one comes home to take up a tiny volume of Grimm and look out at the trees through the little window at the back, one thinks again of women, plants, and lost cosmologies, and realizes that no work of conscious literature or philosophy can last six thousand years. In a mere six pages of Grimm, we have an incredibly moving and profound document of the natural history of life and the cultural history of consciousness. One holds the small volume in one's hand with wonder, as if it were a softly electric piece of amber containing the tiny fossil of an extinct species; and then one feels all around in the orange and thickening air of dusk the amber of slowly congealing time.

CHAPTER TWO

GAIA: COSMOLOGY REGAINED

1. NATURE AND NARRATIVE

"IN THE BEGINNING WAS THE WORD" ARE THE words that begin the Gospel that establishes the quintessentially Western cosmology in which the world is a word, a sound that unfolded space through time. Our word "cosmology" still echoes with the reverberations of that Johannine vision of seven Greek syllables, seven deeply resonant vowels that, like the opening of Bach's *Art of the Fugue,* set forth the theme that has the architecture of its variations implicit within it. From the seven syllables of Creation to the seven seals of the Apocalypse, the story of our world is the sound it makes in its passing. It is only after the opening of the Seventh Seal that there is silence in heaven for the space of half an hour.

In telling the story of once upon a time in gospel, myth, or fairy tale, in returning in the imagination to the time of the *arché,* it is not so much what one says that builds a world, for one can say that the world began in wind or water or word, but

45

it is the telling itself that sets up the structure of identification, the narrative structure that gives form to time and space. When the newly born infant moves its arms and legs in rhythm to its mother's speech,[1] it does not yet know the mother's language, but the sounds themselves set up a relationship of Self and Other that is the fundamental arising of a world.

Poets have known this for some time, and it is for this reason that Wordsworth, in his autobiographical poem, *The Prelude,* began his own phenomenology of mind with the moment in which he is being held at the breast of his nurse, is listening to her song, and hearing it join with the background sounds of the nearby flowing stream, the Derwent. Self and Other are one in this primal state in which milk and music flow into the infant's body, a body that is enveloped in concentric circles by the reverberating bodies of nurse, and stream, and extended space. Through an act of the imagination, the poet is intuiting the very origins of language, the beginning that was the word, for its was most likely the humming and cooing of the nursing mother that imprinted a new generation with the connective power of language. From this primal state of connectiveness and harmony, Wordsworth will grow and fall away into the unhappy consciousness of the alienated mind, and not until the end of the poem, when he is alone on top of Mt. Snowden, will poetic language once again connect him to the sounds of the flowing streams moving down to the horizon of sea and stars. As Wordsworth climbed the mountain, he was lost in the fog, lost in the world of personal mind and abstract social language, but as he persists in his climb, he comes above the fog of the clouds, and suddenly there is the reversal as the medium of alienation in language and fog becomes the medium of connection: now the full moon shines all the more brightly from the reflecting surface of the clouds beneath him, and the sound of the ice melting in all the streams and rushing head-

---

[1] *The Amazing Newborn* (Film, Health Sciences Communications Center, Case Western University, Cleveland, Ohio, 1978).

46

long toward the greater sea seems to echo his own condition in a recursive space in which sea and sky become a single horizon. In this logos of the mind of the poet, a new cosmos is brought forth, one that is neither the innocence of the wordless infant at the breast nor the garrulous man in the city of commerce, but the poetic consciousness in language that participates in the Creation and in the origins of language to re-create an unfallen nature and a renewed culture. Such is the vision of Romanticism, and such is the reason why the nineteenth-century Romantics went to such pains to preserve in literate form the vanishing oral culture of myth and fairy tale.

In a traditional oral culture, the singing first and the telling later present the fundamental epiphany, the worlding that with parent and child recalls the original act of emergence with Creator and creature.

> These my father formerly sang   while carving an axe
>   handle,
> these my mother taught me   while turning her spindle,
> me a child rolling on the floor   in front of her knee,
> miserable milkbeard, little clabbermouth.[2]

The recital of a narrative tells us something about who we think we are, where we think we come from, and where we think we are going. Any narrative, Biblical, Marxist, or Darwinian, that definitively seeks to answer these three questions of: "Who or what are we? Where do we come from? Where are we going?" becomes ineluctably mythopoeic. Technical thinking is narrow and specialized, but mythic thinking is macrothought. Think big and you think myth.

A scientific narrative of the world, from Big Bang to Black Hole, is still a narrative in which the structure is as constituitive of world-making as any particular content. This week the scientists may pontificate with infallibility that the Big

---

[2] *The Kalavala*, Trans. Thomas McGoun (Cambridge, Mass.: Harvard University Press, 1983), p. 8.

Bang is true; next season they may say that in the old days people used to believe in the Big Bang, but now scientists know better and know that Perpetual Creation is the case. And, of course, in the following season, the scientists will make light of the beliefs of the past season, but never will they admit to beliefs or the myth-making that is so basic to the popularization of their science.

When a scientist pushes back from his or her microscope and begins to put the "facts" together in what Wittgenstein called *"die Gesamtheit der Tatsachen,"* he is narratively involving a world that is not merely the collection of things but the entirety of the actually known.[3] This is all the more true when the scientist pushes back from the electron-capture detector to consider, not simply the parts per million of a rare gas, but the atmosphere of the planet as a whole. Parts can rest for a while, content in their partial existence, but when wholes are invoked they bring with them "the patterns that connect," the patterns of narrative, story, and myth. With the emergence of a new way of looking at the whole, called the Gaia hypothesis, the worlds of science and myth have moved ever closer together. From a theoretical apartheid in which an organizing myth put Gallileo in jail to a world in which scientific materialism becomes incapable of explaining the significance of its own findings, we have begun to move in the direction of at least a degree of cohabitation.

2. THE PLAY OF MYTH IN THE WORK OF SCIENCE

THE GAIA HYPOTHESIS proposes that the Earth has been so shaped by life that it makes no sense to look upon the planet as a rock that circles the sun and just happens to carry a

---

[3] See Ludwig Wittgenstein, *Tractatus Logico-Philosophicus* (London: Routledge & Kegan Paul, 1981), p. 30.

thin film of life; rather, we should think of the Earth as a self-regulating entity that can control the salinity of the seas, the temperature of the surface, and the level of oxygen in the atmosphere. From this Gaian perspective, the largest living thing on earth is Earth itself, or herself, if we are to be sensitive to the name "Gaia," which is the ancient Greek name for the goddess of earth and the source for the linguistic root "Ge" from which we derive our words "geometry" and "geography."[4]

All of which is mythic in and of itself, but once we are into Lovelock's text, we find consciously mythic allusions in the imagery of the narrative. Consider Lovelock's reference to Prometheus:

> The countless number and variety of random encounters between individual molecular components of life may have eventually resulted in a chance association of parts which together could perform a lifelike task, such as gathering sunlight and using its energy to contrive some further action which would otherwise have been impossible or forbidden by the laws of

---

[4] When James Lovelock went for a walk in Wiltshire with his neighbor, the novelist William Golding, he described his hypothesis and asked for advice on what to name it. His neighbor, being an artist, not surprisingly suggested calling it "Gaia." Perhaps the artist recognized instinctively that this new hypothesis was in its modern form similar to the shape of something most ancient. In any case, the name had power and brought forth into the world a new relationship between myth and science that was going to trouble people for a decade. It was, however, time, for the simple-minded notions of scientific reductionism were beginning to wear a little thin, and in the 1970s philosophers of science such as Paul Feyerabend, François Jacob, and Michel Serres, were beginning to rearticulate the deep structures that connected myth to science. The landscape for that peripatetic discussion seems enchantingly appropriate, for Wiltshire is the environs of Stonehenge, Old Sarum, and Avebury, and in the seventies it was this mythic landscape of prehistoric Britain that would capture the popular imagination of a generation of children raised on Tolkien and longing as young adults to rediscover the ancient mysteries of Britain in places like Glastonbury and Findhorn. From the children's stories of Alan Garner to the pop archaeology of Michael Dames, stone circles and fairy rings were once again about to reassert their magical visions of a living Earth. And it is precisely with this Western European variant of animism that Evan Wentz discussed in his *The Fairy Faith in Celtic Countries* (London: 1911, 1977) that we have to recall as we consider the ancient cosmology lurking behind the rocks and streams of the Gaia hypothesis.

physics. (The ancient Greek myth of Prometheus stealing fire from heaven and the biblical story of Adam and Eve tasting the forbidden fruit may have far deeper roots in our ancestral history than we realize.)[5]

In his allusions to Greek and Hebrew myths, Lovelock is suggesting that these narratives have a descriptive value that is beyond their literal, fundamentalist interpretations, that they are, in fact, a kind of coded memory of the natural history of life. Although he does not explicitly state his way of reading myth, one can see from the context that, for Lovelock, a myth is an imagistic rendering of events that are more precisely understood when they are translated into the conceptual language of science. The interesting epistemological question that is raised by Lovelock's allusion to the myth of Prometheus is that if we are talking about myth as some sort of cosmic memory, whose memory is it, if the events it remembers antedate the hominization of the primates? If we were not there at the time, who is this Promethean creature, or this archetypal Adam and Eve? If we remember in our myths, who or what is this "we"?

According to one narrative, human beings were not present at the origins of life, and so can have no knowledge of it except through scientific reconstructions. In this straightforward world of what Whitehead called "scientific materialism," mind is epiphenomenal to matter and thoughts are to the brain what urine is to the kidneys. So straightforward and linear is this world view that the proponent is not even aware that he or she is using a simile, for it is precisely simile and metaphor that the materialist is trying to eliminate in reductionism. In this naive philosophy, cultural constructs like "space" and "objects" are taken to be independent of the mind that frames them through its own threshold of possible per-

---

[5] James Lovelock, *Gaia: A New Look at Life on Earth* (New York: Oxford University Press, 1979), p. 14.

ceptions, and by a strange inversion that amounts to a perversion, "mind" and "culture" are reduced to accidental collisions of these imaginary "real" objects in "real" space. This philosophy has a certain innocence that would be childlike and charming, were it not for the fact that this kind of scientific materialism that dominates our universities runs on a subsidy from governments in which the real objects that are put into space are thermonuclear missiles and Star Wars satellites.

The world of scientific materialism is a world we all know only too well; when we distance ourselves from it to consider philosophies considerably more mature, whether they derive from Whitehead or Wittgenstein, we begin to be involved with a different cosmology. If thought is not simply the urine in the brain, and if Mind is immanental in nature such that its pathways, as Gregory Bateson proposed, extend beyond the body,[6] then memory can be one of the modalities of that immanental Mind. We, therefore, remember prehistoric events in myth because "we" as Mind were indeed present. In this more enlightened world of Buddhist relatedness, in this cosmic web of "Indra's Net," the hard and discrete ego simply located in its unconscious projections of objects in space is not all there is to reality.

Myths and fairy tales can therefore remember more than the teller may know. As the stories told under stairs, in kitchens, and in huts, legends and fairy tales are part of the underworld of the conquered and the powerless: of women, children, and artists. As the remains of old mythologies, lost religions, and vanished rituals, the fairy tales can survive only if the implicit is not explicit, for the explicit cosmology is the property of the ruling high priests of the culture. Fairy tales can hold to the past only by hiding it so that what slips in is not recognized by the orthodox who might object to the presence

---

[6] See Gregory Bateson, "Form, Substance, and Difference" in *Steps to an Ecology of Mind* (New York: Ballantine, 1972), p. 461.

of the religion they thought they had supplanted. The strategy of the meek and the powerless has ever been to avoid an open confrontation with the centers of power and to carry on in the hinterlands or on the margins of the culture of the powerful in the lives of children and nursemaids, in the vernacular languages not spoken by the elite, or in the marginal states of consciousness in dream and vision where the imagery of the collective unconsciousness is enduring.

Sometimes it can happen that the ancient persists right alongside the modern, like the remnants of the ancient tallgrass prairie in Kansas that can now only be found alongside the tracks of the railroads, for as the fields were taken over by the monocrops of industrial agriculture, only the flanks of the railroads were left unwalked and uncropped.

And so it is with the orthodox religion of our era, scientific materialism; the old myths and lost cosmologies still linger, and thanks to Romanticism, literary intellectuals know how to find them in the preindustrial cultures that still survive, even in our cities. In the late nineteenth and early twentieth century, A. E. (George William Russell) and Yeats looked to the Irish peasant to teach the London intellectual about the secret truths of nature that lay hidden in the ancient Celtic Fairy Faith; and now in the late twentieth century, anthropologists have turned to African dance, Haitian voodoo, and Yaqui shamanism to show how sex, drugs, and rock and roll are not simply the inventions of a modern electronic society.

There is also another place, one much closer to the power lines of modern science, in which lost mythologies linger and even blossom at the edges of our peripheral vision, and that is in the world of large, all-encompassing scientific theories. The theories have to be large, just as the railroads had to be continental for their tiny margins to be ignored, because only on the scale of the gigantic does the mythic graininess of the texture of reality come into focus. Obviously, the Gaia hypothesis, which moves from the microcosm of the bacteria to the macrocosm of the atmosphere, is one of the larger ideas to come along since Darwinian evolution.

Lovelock and Margulis no longer call Gaia a "hypothesis" but, rather, an evolutionary theory. As a theory, it is part of the new scientific imagination that is concerned with the idea of "emergence" and "emergent properties." In the field of Artificial Intelligence especially, new patterns of what is called "connectionism" have shown how the patterns that connect even dumb units can still express learning, and through energizing and reinforcing pathways that connect neurons or neural nets can begin to show the forms of organization that are essentially cognitive.[7] As an evolutionary theory, Gaia repels scientists who have been trained to think in terms of population biology and the competition of males for leaving the greatest number of offspring, and since Earth is not competing with Venus and Mars for a place in the sun, those scientists who are constrained by the old paradigm can see no selection pressure through which a planetary emergence could evolve. Scientists in the new fields of Artificial Intelligence and planetary dynamics in ocean, atmosphere, and plate tectonics, are much more open to this new narrative of emergent properties and evolution, so it is safe to say that judging Gaia by its enemies as much as by its friends, it is an idea with a future.[8]

Although the theory of Gaia came out of contract research for the California Institute of Technology Jet Propulsion Laboratory's search for life on Mars and has had its publications in the most serious scientific journals, it has been taken up by the counterculture[9] and has inspired a popular *Missa Gaia* by New Age musician Paul Winter as well as various Gaia foundations, societies, and newsletters. This is not all that surprising

---

[7] See Francisco Varela and Evan Thompson, *Worlds Without Ground: Cognitive Science and Human Experience,* Chapter Five, "Emergent Properties and Connectionism," Work in Progress, scheduled for publication in book form in 1990.

[8] See "A Conversation with Lynn Margulis" in *Annals of Earth* (Falmouth, Mass.), Vol. VI, No. 2, August 1988.

[9] Stewart Brand, the creator of the *Whole Earth Catalogue,* was responsible for turning on the counterculture to this scientific work by publishing Lovelock and Margulis's essay, "The Gaia Hypothesis" in his *Co-Evolution Quarterly,* Summer 1975, pp. 30–40.

since "Gaia" as the name of the ancient Greek goddess of the Earth is connected to richly archetypal associations; had the scientists named their hypothesis "The Homeorrhetic Mechanism of Planetary Dynamics," no one would have taken much notice. In invoking the ancient goddess of the Earth, these scientists have summoned up the spirit of myth, and the New Age movement, with its complex ecology of feminism, mysticism, environmentalism, and plain sentimentality, has responded by adopting the hypothesis as one of its own. This adoption, of course, has not helped further its upbringing in the halls of science, and some scientists, such as Richard Dawkins, still insist that the hypothesis is illegitimate and not of true scientific lineage.

The parents of the Gaia theory, however, are indeed legitimate scientists. Dr. James Lovelock is an atmospheric chemist, a Fellow of the Royal Society, and the inventor of the electron-capture detector that enabled scientists to develop the new technology that permits them to study the problems of the Greenhouse Effect and the Ozone Hole. Dr. Lynn Margulis is University Professor in the Department of Botany at the University of Massachusetts at Amherst and is the author of the very influential book, *Symbiosis and Cell Evolution*.[10] It was her point of view of the evolution of the cell that was popularized in Dr. Lewis Thomas's bestseller, *The Lives of a Cell*. But because the Gaia hypothesis is so vast in its scope, the orthodox specialists are not comforted and sense that something sinful must be hiding under the lineaments of the hypothesis, for how else explain its dubious New Age offspring? The Gaia hypothesis is indeed like a foundling left at the threshold, but since the American Geophysical Union decided to make it the subject of its biennial weeklong meeting in San Diego in 1988, there is some indication that the controversial theory is being considered seriously.

---

[10] Lynn Margulis, *Symbiosis and Cell Evolution* (San Francisco: Freeman, 1981).

Scientists, so very much like the rest of us, work through group identifications, snobbery, personal taste, and bias. For the scientific materialists there is something about the Gaia theory that just does not feel right. I will leave it to the scientists themselves to determine whether the theory has any scientific merit, but their culturally allergic reactions to the theory do interest me, for I think that they are indeed sensitive and that what they have picked up on is the presence of narrative structures that are isomorphic to mythopoeic ideas that they have long ago rejected in formulating their materialist world view. Although they have not said it in so many words, the Gaia hypothesis smells like animism, and as we all have known ever since the days of Frazer, animism is a lie, a myth, or, at best, a silly children's fairy tale.

3. GAIAN MYTHS

BUT THE ISOMORPHISM with myth that repelled the Darwinian biologists is precisely what attracted me when I saw Lynn Margulis's films of bacteria for the first time; that is, I could see the world of myth at play within the world of scientific imagery. In 1981, at a meeting of the Lindisfarne Fellows at Zen Center in Marin County, California, Margulis showed her laboratory films of bacteria that served as the visual accompaniment of what was to become her 1984 book, *Early Life*.[11] Appropriately enough, it was in first viewing the ideas of Margulis that I became aware of their visionary company. With all the energy and directness that she can command, Margulis set out to challenge the audience's conventional notion that the world was neatly divided into the parlor game categories of "animal, vegetable, and mineral." Aeons ago, the metabolic processes of bacteria had produced what are now

[11] Lynn Margulis, *Early Life* (Boston: Jones & Bartlett, 1984).

the iron ore deposits in the Gunflint iron formations of Minnesota and Western Ontario, and the excretions of cyanobacteria had produced the oxygen that formed the atmosphere we now breathe. So from the earth below to the sky above, the world as we know it has been shaped by bacteria.

As Lynn spoke of the iron ore deposits, my mind flashed with movies of my own as I saw dwarves working in the mines, and recalled the Disney film of *Snow White* that I had seen as a child of five. What kind of intuition was it, I wondered, that enabled the teller of fairy tales to suggest that there were little creatures at work in the mines underneath our surface life?

To show just how formative of this earth the bacteria truly were, Margulis went on to show pictures of stromatolites in Australia, those fossils of microbial mats from billions of years ago, and emphasized how early it was that life appeared on this Earth and just how much the planetary dynamics of our world had been shaped by it for three and one half billion years. Clearly, Lynn wanted us to respect these not-so-cute little buggers that were everywhere around us, on us, and in us. Then she zoomed in on the teeming life of a colony of spirochetes attached to larger cells. Astonishing to me was the complexity of their movements: the spirochetes oscillated in such a way that when one looked at the entire group of them one saw standing wave patterns shimmering in a lovely crystalline geometry that looked more like an electron microscope photograph of an ion than a swarm of the kind of bacteria that could also give us syphilis. Here was the problem of the One and the Many in a new Platonic visionary dialogue, for at the "physical" level of the "real," there were only bits of protoplasm, but at the mental level of the Batesonian "pattern that connects" there were geometries and, most likely, in the three dimensions of the solution, complex topologies of pure form. In Margulis's film I was looking at Plato's Sensible and Intelligible realms, the realms of matter and the realms of mind. And as one considered the rodlike shape of the unassociated and freely ranging spirochete, and watched it pulse back and forth like a plucked string in vibration, one could observe the harmonics that had attracted Pythagoras when he discovered the relationship between the length of the string and the pitch. "Study the monochord" are the legendary last words of Pythagoras and as one looked at the plucked string of the spirochete one could see in that monochord the vibratory harmonics that must have been constitutive of the patterns of association responsible for the origins of life.

The hour of Margulis's lecture was over in a psychedelic instant, and as we went out of the room onto the deck for coffee and tea, my mind was swarming with the interior life of my own images and childhood recollections. Filled with the enthusiasm of discovery, I went over to Francisco Varela and started babbling of dwarves in the mines in Disney and angels in the Islamic NeoPlatonism of Henri Corbin. *"Que me quedé balbuciendo/Toda sciencia transcendiende."*[12] And babbling I must have been, and certainly transcending science, for Varela looked at me with puzzlement and frustration and said: *"¡Ay que Thompson! No puedo hacer nada con eso. Soy científico!"*

My friendship with Varela was such that I felt only a little rebuffed and I let him have the space he needed to pursue a more technical discussion with Humberto Maturana, Lynn Margulis, and Heinz Pagels. Savoring my private sense of intellectual excitement, I moved over to the balcony's edge and looked out into the evening darkness toward a clump of cypress trees and beyond in the direction of the Pacific ocean, which was only a short distance away. The landscape in my mind was changing, and the concern with myth and prehistory that had absorbed me in my just published book, *The Time Falling Bodies Take to Light,* was shifting farther back in time to focus on the truly mythic horizon of the prehistory of life on Earth.

---

[12] Lines from the poem of St. John of the Cross, *"Entréme donde no supé"* or "Verses Written Upon an Ecstasy of High Contemplation."

After the break, we returned to the room to continue for another hour or so of discussion, but I did not attempt to try out my wild ideas with the group, so I pursued my own line of private thoughts as Maturana, Varela, Lovelock, Heinz von Foerster, and Heinz Pagels kept the discussion going in a legitimately scientific manner.

Varela must have sensed that he had been too summarily dismissive of my free associations, for the next morning at breakfast, before the morning session, he came over to me on the deck, where we all were once again assembled for coffee, and said: "You know, it's funny about what you said last night. This morning I had a dream. Once again I was looking at Lynn's film of the spirochete, and I was seeing the 'intelligible realm' of the Platonic geometry you talked about last night, but this time I could hear the music that the vibrating undulipodia were making, and it was unbelievably beautiful. It was like Bach or the music of the spheres, a kind of perfect knowledge, and then I awoke in a state of complete and absolute cognitive bliss."

It was typical of Varela's Latin generosity that he came over so quickly to make up for the easy dismissal of the night before, as if to apologize that he had been so momentarily caught up in the discussions with his scientific colleagues that my poetic ravings had been an insensitive intrusion, a form of discourse that was not appropriate to the language of science, as indeed it was not. It was also typical of Varela's imagination that he could make the shift from one hemisphere of the brain to the other in a single night. Most scientists take a lifetime for such a transformation, and Darwin lamented at the end of his life that he wished he had spent more time with music and art and less time being a machine for grinding out facts; but Varela, open as he was to music and meditation, needed only a night to have a dream that was itself a continuation of the Platonic dialogue of the conference as a whole. Almost as if in answer to my unspoken question as to how the spirochetes could coordinate their movements to achieve such beautiful collective geometry, Varela's dream came as the answer. They achieved their geometry through the resonance of vibration and music; those crowded bacteria that were to become our very own undulipodia (spermtails and oviductilia) were not only instruments of motion, they were also instruments of sound and music.

In Lovelock's talk to the Fellows, and in his book, he spoke of the death of the binary star that occurred before our solar system was formed, of how we all carried in our bodies the atomic material of a dead star. Once again my mind transposed concepts into imagery and I thought of the esoteric Christian vision of the mystical body of Christ, of the cosmic being who says: "Take, eat: this is my body." (Luke 14:22) What was expressed in the eucharist was a vision in which all life is food for one another, from exploding stars to the soft rain of dead diatoms in the seas, "the tests" that produce those layers of chalk at the sea's bottom that serve to sink calcium carbonate and thereby control the levels of salinity of the oceans. This religious vision of the web of life and death is not restricted to Christianity or Judaism, for the Upanishads also give voice to this sense of planetary connectiveness:

Earth is food. Air lives on earth. Earth is air. Air is Earth. They are food to one another.

For Lovelock, the emergence of what we know as air was one of the greatest events of pollution in the history of the planet, for the excretions of the photosynthesizing bacteria accumulated as a poison to the anerobes and they had to retreat from those who fed on light and oxygen to sink down into the darkness of the slime at the bottom of lakes or deep into the guts of the living creatures who came to supplant them. Here was the war of the *devas,* the creatures of light, against the *asuras,* the demons of darkness in Hindu mythology; here was the war of Michael the Archangel fighting against Satan and driving him down to chain him to the underworld.

Margulis spoke of the great divide, the gulf that separated the prokaryotic bacteria from our own eukaryotic cells. In one there was a single planetary bioplasm in which reproduction and the exchange of genetic material was not linked to sex and death; in the other was a world of distinct individuals who reproduced themselves through mitotic sexuality and died. Individuality, sexuality, and death: were not these the very things that religious orders objected to and tried to escape in their wish to reachieve "the sacred" that was, in actuality, not the imagined prophetic future, but the most ancient past of the prehistory of life?

Differing world views bring forth differing cultures and systems of knowledge, and we do not appreciate their complexity and insights, if we simply rank them in a linear developmental system of inferior and superior. Every technology has its light and its shadow, and Avebury is not simply a primitive version of the Mauna Loa observatory in Hawaii. A linear accelerator can be seen to be as clumsy and needlessly complicated an instrument as a megalithic stone circle, and both can be appreciated to bring forth forms of knowledge that the other lacks. If we begin to understand that our ancestors did have intelligence and a sensitivity to wind and weather, plants and planets, then we can begin to appreciate that for a preindustrial culture, one endowed with perceptual acuity and imagination, but no microscopes or telescopes, that a feeling for the life at their feet in the leafmold could easily transform itself into images of half-human elves and fairies, salamanders and ondines, sprites and nymphs, trolls and goblins. In fact, one can now make a case that this animistic vision is more scientific than the industrial Pasteur vision of bacteria in which the modern suburban housewife tries to protect her family from germs by spraying the air inside the home with carcinogenic disinfectants. The "little people" are indeed half-human, for they are, as anaerobes, inside our guts, but as they are also, according to Sonea and Panisset, a planetary bioplasm,[13] it is

---

[13] See Sorin Sonea and Maurice Panisset, *A New Bacteriology* (Boston: Jones & Bartlett, 1983), p. 8.

just as accurate to say that we are little creatures inside them. And if the Chain of Being goes on, and we are only the end of it because we are blind to anything that is beyond us, then perhaps Plato's Intelligible Realms are filled with those creatures of pure Mind and Music that used to be called angels. Just as bacteriology has brought us face to face with ancient animism, perhaps Artificial Intelligence, that world of abstract topologies, will bring us face to face with creatures who are even more bodiless than Max Headroom, creatures of pure topology that the ancients lovingly catalogued as angels, archangels, powers, thrones, dominions, cherubim, and seraphim. Perhaps one of the more seriously interesting questions for modern topology or Witten's String Theory of ten-dimensional physics is: "How many angels can dance on the head of a pin?"

Above us in the food chain may be angels, below us may be goblins and fairies. And in the ancient Fairy Faith there is quite a difference between the two, for goblins are nasty creatures of the dark who dislike humans for having usurped their world, but fairies can be helpful for those sensitive souls who are not so concerned with only human matters. If we translate from the visual language of animism to the conceptual language of biology, then the goblins are the anaerobic bacteria who live on and in our wastes and garbage, and the fairies, those airy creatures of light, are the cyanobacteria that were the first to invent photosynthesis to feed on light to give off the oxygen that would become the new atmosphere of an illuminated world. The fairies, as cyanobacteria, are the transitional creatures between elementals (the prokaryotes) and humans (the eukaryotes) and hold implicit in their evolution the differentiation that will become the new world order of plants and animals; but as the most ancient cyanobacteria are still prokaryotic (without a cellular nucleus), they lack our specific genetic individuality and are pansexual in that they do not reproduce through the sexual splitting of mitosis, but in their ability to serve as the foundation of a new world order,

they are enormously attractive and contain the sexual magne-
tism of both the male and the female. And so in our stories
that are forms of cultural storage for the natural history of life
we tell of how the fairies lived before the age of man and
brought light to a darkened world.

If all these mythological images have references that can
run parallel to the stream of concepts in scientific narratives,
then what is the nature of knowledge in this more ancient
form of "seeing," this way of knowing through imagery that
we still call the imagination?

4. SUPERSTITIONS—PSYCHIC AND SCIENTISTIC

IN MANY WAYS, the counterculture of the 1960s and the
New Age movement of the 1970s and 1980s are not new at all,
but are simply continuations of the line of work of Blake, Col-
eridge, Wordsworth, Goethe, Bergson, Yeats, Steiner, Whitehead, and Aldous Huxley. When one looks back at such a
heady lineage of geniuses, it is rather astonishing to consider
that the dominant culture of today, expressed in such journals
as the *New York Review of Books* or through academic and safely
tenured critics like Christopher Lasch, can regard these movements as anti-intellectual and only concerned with psychic
channeling and occult healing with purple crystals.[14]

Imagination, for the line of thinking that moves from Col-
eridge and Goethe up to Steiner and Yeats, represents a different mode of participatory perception—a different way of
being in the world. This kind of perception is not simply another word for deception. Perhaps I can elucidate the change
in attitude that is needed to move from a postmodernist sensibility in which myth is regarded as an absolute and au-

---

[14] See Christopher Lasch's review of the New Age movement in *Omni,* October
1987.

thoritarian system of discourse to a planetary culture in which myth is understood to be isomorphic, but not identical, to scientific narratives, by presenting my own difficulties in coming to appreciate, for example, the animism of Rudolph Steiner.

When I first read Rudolph Steiner's *Cosmic Memory,* I could only take it in as a form of mysticism that had absolutely nothing to do with science. It was its own world, very much like science fiction, and, like science fiction, it could have various poetic truths, but one could not take its narratives as descriptions of our conventional world. Actuality, however, was just what Steiner was claiming for himself in his project of "reading" the "akashic record." What, then, was one to make of descriptions of stages in human evolution in which the human body floated in the sea, or was not yet male and female but produced offspring singly from within itself, or was cold-blooded. Not even Sir Alastair Hardy's theory of the aquatic hominids that has been popularized by Elaine Morgan could fit the bizarre anthropology that Steiner proposed.

Steiner described evolution on the planets and talked about the separation of the sun and moon from the earth and a stage of evolution on Saturn, but it was obvious from his descriptions that these places were dimensions and not simply planets out there in space, and, in fact, one could not think of dimensions and space in the normal way and make any sense of the way he explained things. One had to put Steiner in a separate file along with Cayce, Tolkien, and Castaneda, or with all the other alternative cosmologies that my generation of the 1960s liked to collect.

At that time, I was an instructor of humanities at Massachusetts Institute of Technology, and in the conventional world view of science there was only one way of looking at things. Thanks to Jacques Monod, we knew that everything was simply a product of chance. Life was an accidental, slimy coating on the hunk of rock that was Earth, and Earth was a not very significant planet in the backwater provinces of a galaxy. Culture was epiphenomenal to nature, and the mind was epiphenomenal to brain. What was real was stuff, and stuff was "out there." Out there was reality, and you had to adjust to it, for that was what "adaptation" was all about. But out there was also the war in Vietnam and the ecological crisis, and so I began to think that we weren't adapting to an independent reality but were creating a world out of our illusions, creating innumerable problems out of all our technological "solutions." If illusions could create a world, if the miseducation of engineers could generate planetary pollution, and if the technocrats as "the Best and the Brightest" could lead us toward annihilation in the defense of abstractions, then perhaps, I thought, it was time to consider that the generation of illusions had something to teach us about the creation of reality, or realities.[15]

So, my generation went shopping for alternative realities and ransacked all human history. We rummaged about in shamanism, Zen, yoga, Tibetan Buddhism, Rudolph Steiner, Edgar Cayce, Stonehenge, flying saucers, dolphins, science fiction, and whatever else could serve to create virtual reality through the virtue of not being "real" according to the tenured professors of the established culture. It was a nice division of "us" and "them," of hippies and doves versus straights and hawks. There was mysticism and there was science, and you could either stay on at Berkeley and MIT, or take acid, drop out, go to India, or take up life on a hippie commune.

That was the 1960s. But in the 1970s, things began to become less polarized as the scientists became more mystical and the mystics more scientific. At places like Esalen in California or Lindisfarne in New York, David Finkelstein was discussing the mind in quantum physics, Gregory Bateson was discussing the mind in nature, arguing that "the organism plus the environment" was the unit of evolution, and Francisco Varela was maintaining that "adaptation" in evolutionary theory was

---

[15] See W. I. Thompson, *At the Edge of History* (New York: Harper & Row, 1971).

64

as questionable a reification as the concept of "representation" in cognitive science.[16]

Because science has now changed, so has mysticism. There is now more intellectual elbow room for us all, and the diversity of small institutions, such as the Santa Fe Institute for the Study of Complexity, the Dynamical Systems Collective in Santa Cruz, or the Rocky Mountain Institute in Snowmass, Colorado, has opened up new windows in our minds. If now one goes back to Steiner and reads him, not with the mindset of the counterculture of the 1960s, but with the creative science of the 1980s, from ten-dimensional String Theory to Gaian geophysiology, then the narratives take on a new life. There is no such thing as "matter" or "stuff"; matter is a cultural abstraction. There is no such thing as "out there," for that flat dimensionality is simply a conventional way of bracketing out complexity to empower a social consensus that has tacitly agreed not to perceive anything outside its frame. And so, if Steiner chooses to look at the evolution of the solar system and sees ways in which the planets are not hunks of stuff out there but nodes of vibration that resonate in multiple dimensions that enfold themselves into one another in patterns of complex recursiveness in which Sun, Moon, and Saturn are also modalities of Earth, then he is not raving but is expanding our notions of cosmology. If he talks about the human body floating in the sea, and after the integration of the "I" still having a number of parts that were still on the plant level, he is talking about the human body as the evolution of the eukaryotic cell and the vestigial plant parts as the organelles, such as the mitochondria. If Steiner says, "Thus the first likenesses of man were eaters of animals and of men," he is far back in time with the amoebas and protists, just as when he is talking about how "every human being could pro-

---

[16] See Francisco Varela, "Laying Down a Path in Walking" in *Gaia, A Way of Knowing: Political Implications of the New Biology* (Great Barrington, Mass.: Lindisfarne Press, 1987), pp. 48–65.

duce another human being out of himself," he is talking about life at the state of the prokaryotic cell.

That this is not the normal way of looking at evolution is obvious even to a father taking his child to visit the Boston Museum of Science. There, as one goes in to see the display of dinosaurs, one is met with a sign that says: "No human ever saw these, for dinosaurs lived seventy million years before Man." But if one sees humanity after the manner of Steiner, then that statement is incorrect: we were the dinosaurs, just as once we were the prokaryotic cells. Steiner's identification with the biosphere is so total that the whole story is "our" story.

The Steinerian vision is one that looks at the human as so completely embedded in the animal, vegetal, and mineral evolution of the solar system that it becomes nonsense to separate a fictive "matter" from mind, and a mere three dimensions from ten, or to talk confidently about "chance" when one does not perceive the pattern that connects three dimensions to ten. Here, Cabbalistic mysticism, rather than being nonsense, becomes tensense. It becomes a biology, a *bios logos* that brings events together in a much more extensive narrative of life. All of the seemingly mystical perceptions of Steiner have a biological relevance that fits a new kind of science, and a new kind of culture. But Steiner did not get his information from his colleagues, and his followers now tend to be humorless, rigid, and doctrinaire, so how can one accept a "science of the spirit" that speaks about clairvoyant vision and ends up in yet another cult? If we try to avoid the errors in thinking of the dominant academic institutions, we seem to fall into yet another set of errors in subcultures and cults.

If the dominant institutions dismiss the mythic and the symbolic, the subculture seems to respond by insisting on taking the mythic and symbolic literally. Mediums and psychic channels have again become popular; it is now even fashionable for yuppies on Wall Street to go to psychics for readings, and even President Reagan consulted his astrologer. (However, considering the dubious record of "the dismal science" of economics, perhaps he is better off with astrologers than economists, for at least they are looking at a world of planets and not a set of abstractions that have no environmental life, such as the Gross National Product.) It is probably to be expected that when an intensely materialistic culture becomes interested in the spiritual, it will do so in a manner in which the spiritual is experienced as another form of technological materialism with its gadgetry of crystals, radionics, and pyramid power. In both cases of materialism and psychism, the same category-mistake seems to dominate as multiple dimensions are smashed down into a fundamentalist kind of literalism. In many ways, the psychic channel seems to function as a kind of trash compactor for the astral plane or collective unconscious. Whatever dream scraps are floating around, from flying saucers, lost continents, earthquakes, and catastrophes, are seized upon by the medium who can dream and sleeptalk, and compact the trash into an idol to collect a group of admirers and supporters.

The sociology of these psychic messages has not varied much since the flying saucer contactee cults of the 1950s; the technique still preferred is to magnetize a group through fear of some imminent catastrophe, be it war or earthquake, and then propose that the listeners who are privileged to have access to the medium are the chosen few who will survive into the new age, *if* they follow instructions. And, of course, the instructions usually have to do with joining the cult, moving to a safe place, and making donations to the cause. The glamor of being chosen by extraterrestrials for seeding a new line of human evolution has a certain sex appeal, and these active dramas are a bit more involving than watching television, so it is not surprising that they succeed in drawing followings. What is intriguing, however, is that when the predictions fail to come true on the appointed day, neither the channel nor the followers experience a crisis of confidence, for they simply shift the dates forward and claim that because of the power of the followers' meditations, the world was saved, and the apocalypse has been delayed. It is indeed a clever strategy, one not unlike the fears put into us by the military–industrial complex, for if bad things happen, the fearful prophecy is confirmed, and if nothing happens, the fearful prophecies are also confirmed by the success of our defense system. Such was the case for the psychic predictions of the televized Second Coming of Christ for 1984, prophesied by Benjamin Cream, or of the galactic Harmonic Convergence of 1987, prophesied by José Argüelles.

Psychism seems to be a democratization of paranoia, and paranoia is a way of misunderstanding the poetry of language. The paranoid will say things like: "Extraterrestrials have placed a radio in my skull and they are beaming messages to me from Sirius." Translated from the code, this could be rendered as: "I am more important than people realize and have a hidden value that is not being recognized in my social situation. I have a soul and this extends beyond the physical realm into other dimensions." And, of course, from a spiritual and compassionate point of view, all of this may very well be true. Most paranoid utterances or psychic channelings do have a certain descriptive power as political caricatures. If paranoids claim that there is a conspiracy controlling world events, it does serve to recognize that the shallow explanations in the news never really express the hidden connectiveness of events. The larger cultural transformations of history are invisible from the perspective of the daily news, and the complex simultaneities of seemingly separated events often have a network of interactions and complex feedback loops that only a god or a paranoid could detect. Paranoids, like artists, can sense what they do not know, but unlike artists, they have no social and intellectual way of dealing with their perceptions.

The artist, in contrast to the psychic channel, renders the spirit into the contextual frame of the physical, but the artist knows that he or she is being symbolic. Dreams and visions are like monetary currency: by adopting a conventional symbolic value they bring a consensual domain into being, a world economy and culture. The ontology rests with the emergent domain and not with the image of the king on the coin or the President on the paper. The psychic turns the paper into an icon filled with *mana* or vibrations, and as a paranoid perception of the implicit power of a monetary instrument to precipitate a consensual domain, this perception is not completely incorrect. But psychics, paranoids, and fundamentalist followers of any persuasion keep committing the same category mistake over and over again. The acid test is that all paranoids and fundamentalists lack a sense of humor, for humor is a chaos dynamic of flux and flexability, of ambiguity and multidimensionality, and that kind of erotic liveliness is precisely what the fundamentalist is trying to eliminate in holding rigidly to doctrine. Look at the faces of the Ayatollah Khomeini, Ian Paisley, the Pope, Rabbi Kahane, and Jimmy Swaggart. Personally, I distrust those who frown a lot when they pray: they look as if they are in pain and are about to inflict their pain on others.

"The difference that makes a difference" between the metanoid and the paranoid, or between the mystic and the psychotic, is that psychotic individuals are in a state of pain and terror in which their identities are being crushed by the overload of information and complexity of "the world." The artist and the mystic know that you don't have to drink the ocean to swim in it; consequently, complexity does not engulf them.

There seems to be a cycle to knowing in the manner in which various subcultures interact within a culture. The general level of accepted reality or normalcy can be called *nous*. As *nous* moves through the space and time of a culture, it decays into *noise*. As noise accumulates, it generates an information overload and an epistemological disorientation that stimulates *paranoia*. These paranoid caricatures of pattern recognition, however, are of interest to the artist, the cultural historian, or the philosopher and can serve as data for descriptions of changes of state in the culture at large, so paranoia becomes data for the next level up in *metanoia*. Metanoia, if favored by the circumstances of history, can become the new condition of normalcy, and thus metanoia stabilizes itself as *nous,* and the cycle keeps on turning as this *nous* decays into *noise.* From the point of view of Egypt, Moses was a paranoid, but from the point of view of Israel, Moses was a metanoid. From the point of view of the Catholic Church, Descartes was a paranoid, suffering from weird dreams and delusions of grandeur that alienated him from the common reality of the time; but from the point of view of the newly emergent world view of science, Descartes was a metanoid who helped to effect a change in state of our civilization and thus created a new definition of *nous.* Now, of course, science has been so thoroughly routinized that *nous* has decayed into *noise,* and we are once again awash with paranoias of innumerable varieties, from José Argüelles[17] to Lyndon Larouche. And so the wheel of knowledge keeps on spinning: Nous > Noise > Paranoia > Metanoia > Nous > Noise > Paranoia > Metanoia.

Myth is, therefore, a way of using language that can express both metanoia and paranoia, depending on the manner in which the individual relates to the experience of multi-dimensionality. When rendered into the imagery and points of reference of our concrete, three-dimensional world, myth is

---

[17] For a textbook example of paranoid cosmic synthesis, see José Argüelles's *Earth Ascending* (Boulder, Col.: Shambala Books, 1984). Over the years of receiving many strange letters and documents, I have noticed that paranoid letters and manuscripts often have Einstein in the first sentence, for he seems to serve as an archetypal symbol of self-validation. The letters very often will have no margins, or margins in which another line of text is added: it is as if open space is a threat or a blank screen that immediately fills up with projections. Nothing must be left loose and unconnected in these cosmic narratives. This book was shortly withdrawn from circulation by the embarrassed publisher, and this, of course, only feeds the paranoid sense that the world is out to suppress the hidden truths the seer has detected. In succeeding in making his "Harmonic Convergence" (in which the Earth was returned to the Galactic Central Command, the cosmic source from which the Maya Indians derived their knowledge) a global event, one that was reported on Chinese television and the front page of the *International Herald Tribune* as well as in the comic strips of Doonesbury, Dr. Argüelles dramatically embodies the complex and ambiguous sociology of knowledge that validates a Moses or a Descartes.

a Platonic "likely story" that helps us to remember spiritually who we are, where we come from, and where we are meant to go. The narrower world of compulsory socialization can restrict us by seeking to rob us of this other identity and frame of reference: it replaces a world view with an ideology empowered by the thought police of a temporary elite. Because mythic knowledge has a way of delegitimating elites, it is socially threatening and has traditionally been kept as esoteric knowledge for the stable few who are not likely to become psychotic. Indeed, if we look back over the last quarter century of the drugged counterculture, we can see that there is much wisdom in keeping the esoteric esoteric. But the genie is out of the bottle, and all the old secret oral teachings are now available in paperback. Perhaps this planetization of the esoteric is itself a cultural indication that this psychic level of mental evolution is over and we are preparing to leap in a new direction. Like the explosion of Renaissance magic that preceded the emergence of science and the modernist mentality, this so-called "New Age" is probably the swan song of all the old ages.

But our modernist mentality is also at its end, and as it ends it is breaking in two. We now have a choice between the literalism of scientific materialism or the literalism of psychic materialism. If we flee from the reductionism of academic cults such as sociobiology, we may just find ourselves moving in the direction of other equally American cults in which the psychic is marketed as kitsch.[18]

Every culture generates its shadow: normalcy sustains mediocre bureaucracies and charismatic innovation creates cults. Leaders create followers, and followers mechanically copy the

---

[18] In 1971, Findhorn was a small New Age village in Scotland that made a name for itself by outrageously claiming that it was by "attuning to the fairies and the elemental kingdom" that enabled them to grow giant cabbages in sand. Now the visitor to Kraft's agribusiness and junk food pavilion at EPCOT in Disney World can take a ride in a boat past plastic devas that shake their leafy hands and sing, "Attune to the Land! Attune to the Land!"

letter and miss the spirit. Almost by some tragic kind of Greek "Necessity," leaders will generate the pathology of followership, but, paradoxically, evil leaders will expose their rottenness faster and thus force the liberation of their benighted dupes more quickly, but good men can hold followers in thralldom for decades, even centuries. Clearly, the cultural contradictions that are built into any revitalization movement are quite difficult, perhaps even tragically unresolvable at the human level. Neither Moses, Buddha, Christ, nor Mohammed seems to have solved the problem. Act like a Messiah and you will be killed. (Exit Ché Guevara.) Act like a Cassandra, and you will be ignored. (Exit Rachel Carson.) Act like a leader and you will get followers who will degrade your ideas. (Exeunt omnes.) But if degradation is a natural process, one like anaerobic digestion, then perhaps the hucksters have a more compassionate feeling for the masses than the elitist purist who tries to protect himself from contamination and infection by wearing a sterile mask as he walks the streets. Perhaps those who take material with the purpose of degrading it are like farmers working with compost; they prove that the season for this organic matter is over, that the *kairos* for that expression is finished, and so by turning it over in piles of degrading matter they prepare the soil for those who follow with new seeds. The mediums, psychic channels, and movie stars help everyone to see that the psychic is atavistic, an evolutionary dead end, and merely reruns of past lives in old movies, places we have been and not visions of where we are going.

Perhaps this cultural phenomenology is basic to the human level, and that what we can learn from the Gaian evolutionary theory, or from Steiner's total identification with the planetary dynamics of life, is that this human level is itself unstable, limited, and transitional. There is no way to fix things up culturally or politically as long as you are going to have human beings in the solution. Robert Muller says that the United Nations has a list of world problems of some 20,000 items needing immediate attention. If culture is inherently limited and flawed, then it is a bit naive to think that human cultures will eliminate automobiles to save the atmosphere, quit smoking, or rid themselves of poverty and wars. This hominid moment is not a state that can be perfected; it is a process, and to arrest that process is probably not possible, even if we tried to stop time and make the planet eternally comfortable for human life. Once we were prokaryotic bacteria, then we were dinosaurs, and now we are humans about to become, through a catastrophic bifurcation, subhuman and posthuman, or God only knows what else. What is creating this something else is a complex phenomenology in which both the human good and the human evil are tearing human culture apart. From the greenhouse effect to the ozone hole, or from sex, drugs, and rock and roll to fundamentalist purifications, or from genetic engineering to artificial intelligence, everything we like to call human and home, even the planet as we have known it, is being taken from us by our own actions, conscious and unconscious. From this posthuman point of view, "the new planetary culture" that I have written about in, I suppose, too optimistic a way, should be seen more tragically as the period of disintegration of all traditional human cultures, tribal, religious, national, and racial. Just as cyanobacteria created a "polluted" atmosphere, or cattle overgraze to create deserts, so humans seem intent on overdeveloping their niche so that it can explode into the bifurcation that produces the novel and the unthinkable.

Interestingly enough, the parents of the Gaia hypothesis both see our present culture as one that is on its way out. From their perspective of planetary dynamics, however, they see two quite different finales. Lynn Margulis sees the inevitable evolution of new life forms, including the replacement of human carbon-based life with a silicon-based life of machines.[19] James Lovelock sees Gaia reasserting its prefered

---

[19] See Lynn Margulis and Dorion Sagan, "Gaia and the Evolution of Machines," *Whole Earth Review*, No. 55, Summer 1987, pp. 15–21.

temperature in a new Ice Age,[20] one that will decimate the human population levels of the moment.

Although we humans have very good reasons for not being comfortable with these catastrophic points of view, it is hard to avoid them if one thinks on the macroscopic level of cosmology or myth. Astrophysics has given us narratives of Big Bangs, Black Holes, colliding galaxies and supernovae, and myth has simply given us different names for these events. In the Middle Earth between science and myth, Rudolph Steiner has left us narratives of cosmic memory that have the "pralayas" or catastrophes that give the punctuated equilibrium of evolution a chance for rest and innovation. At one level, these Gaian catastrophes are tragic and terrifying, but at another level, they are comforting and affirming, for if once "we" were prokaryotic bacteria and dinosaurs, and here "we" are again as hominids lately turned human, then existence is a process in which death is a necessary release from premature crystallizations that would stop time to lock us into an illusion that we thought was reality. Both myth and science seem to agree on an ontology in which the universe is catastrophically transformative, from the supernova of the binary star to the Cretaceous Extinction. If science is telling us the truth, then myth has not been lying to us about the war in heaven.

But an isomorphism is not an identity, so it is important to appreciate the differences between myth and science. Myth is a horizon that surrounds a location or a definition: it is not itself the measurement in that location. We can have various mythologies of science, such as the scientific socialism of Trotsky and Lenin, or the positivism of Comte, the behaviorism of Skinner, or the sociobiology of Wilson, but we never can have a science of myth, for myth is always the relationship between the known and the unknown. It is the hori-

---

[20] See "A Conversation with James Lovelock," *Annals of Earth* (Falmouth, Mass.), Vol. 5, No. 3, December 1987, p. 9.

zon of science itself where technologies fail and we are left not to our own devices, but to our own ontology. Here we can no longer read a meter to take a measurement, we can only fall back on the way in which we know that we know. When Descartes moved into this science fiction landscape at the edge of science, even he slipped into meditations that were disguised gnostic myths about the deceiving spirit, an imaginary being who was the epistemological mask of the Evil Demiurge.

An ecology requires the balance that comes from diversity, marshes and deserts, oceans and continents, and it is the same for an ecology of mind. If one single ideology were to triumph to become a monocrop, it would be monstrous and generate a "complexity catastrophe" that would be needed to maintain the openness to innovation that is basic to life. In many ways the psychism of a J. Z. Knight or a Shirley MacLaine is isomorphic to the scientism of a B. F. Skinner or an E. O. Wilson, for both represent multidimensional ontologies that have been squashed down into flat ideologies of power and control. When science delivers us from scientism, it expands to regain its full multidimensionality and its sense of intellectual balance: and when spirituality delivers us from psychism, it, too, expands to regain its sense of wisdom and compassionate universality.

5. IMAGINATION AND SCIENCE

IF ONE OBSERVES the play of myth in the work of science it does not mean that science does not work and that one should simply surrender to the irrational. Just as aesthetics has its role to play in mathematical elegance but still cannot replace the demands of verification, so the mythopoeic has its role to play in sensitizing us to the complexity of narratives and the multidimensionality of existence, but it cannot take the place of scientific research. A hypothesis can be proved wrong, and we may decide no longer to accept the idea of phlogiston, but a myth cannot be disproved; it can only lose its suggestiveness and its capacity to startle the imagination. We can disprove alchemy as a scientific hypothesis, but this is a category mistake: it is like trying to take Santa Claus's weight in kilos. Alchemy as a mythopoeic narrative that relates the evolution of consciousness to the evolution of nature is a symbolic system that Jung rescued from the trash heap of Western science. Alchemy is not disproved, any more than Sumerian mythology is disproved. What is always disproved is the "misplaced concreteness" in which the lead is claimed about to be turned into gold, or the Santa Claus in front of Saks Fifth Avenue is claimed to be *the* Santa Claus, or the Rajneesh in the Rolls Royce is claimed to be divine. If one understands that all life on Earth carries the matter of a dead star, then the transformation of nature into culture, of grain into bread and of grapes into wine, is a performance of a profound mystery of the evolution of life: if one thinks that in taking communion, one is literally chewing on the flesh and blood of Jesus, then it is easy to disprove the contention by placing the eucharistic host under a microscope. Khruschev sent up an astronaut to look for God, and failing to find him, claimed that God did not exist, but one needs to remember that what one is disproving in such tests is not the myth, but the category mistake.

One can indeed test the Gaia hypothesis through specific projects of research, such as studying the relationships between plankton in the ocean and the atmospheric stabilization of the global climate,[21] but one cannot prove it by having dreams or visions of fairies and angels, or of Gaia herself, though these dreams and visions can certainly motivate the scientist to look in new places or make new connections, as Kékulé did when he had his dream of the serpent biting its tail and then *reworked* the image into the scientific concept of the benzene ring.

---

[21] See Richard Monastersky, "The Plankton-Climate Connection" in *Science News*, Vol. 132, No. 23, December 5, 1987, pp. 362–365.

What the isomorphism of myth and science can teach us is that when the horizons of science shift dramatically, that movement stimulates the opening of an expanded space that by its scale alone becomes mythopoeic in its multidimensionality. The Gaia hypothesis is just such a transformation of imagery that opens us up to the Imagination. If with this newly stimulated imagination we see connections between animism and Gaian science, it does not mean that we are simply regressing to prescientific modes of thought. In the rise of secular modernism, we moved away from traditionally religious modes of thought to see matter as dead and mind as divorced from nature. Now in the shift from European modernism to a planetary culture, we see that that ideology was too simplistic, that there are intriguing relationships between myth and science and that animism contains some intuitive insights that are worth exploring in the *differing* ways of art, science, and philosophy.

The reductionist manner of responding to the isomorphism between animism and Gaian science would be to try to hold on to the old modernist mentality by saying, "The elementals are nothing but bacteria, fairies are nothing but cyanobacteria, and angels are nothing but the messengers of viruses." Once again, multidimensionality would be compressed into flatness. The new mentality, however, is not the "nothing butness" of reductionism but a vision of interpenetrating worlds. In the medieval world of traditionally sacred cultures, Christian, Judaic, or Islamic, angels are "up there." There is a split universe, split between the sacred and the profane, heaven and earth. In a planetary culture, there is an appreciation of the interpenetration of dimensions, an infolding in which the transcendent is immanent. In this new world view, a virus or a bacterium would be the tip of an iceberg, the apex of a triangle whose tip is in our "world," but whose multidimensional extensiveness can take it into other "worlds."

A world is the contextual framing of an observer: the

spirochete that is giving us syphilis may be vibrating its music in other dimensions and not be so exclusively defined by our world. A virus that may be carrying genetic messages at the cellular level may be involved in narratives of evolution that are invisible to the organism and only perceptible at the level of the species and its emergent evolutionary landscape. Such a creature may indeed be imagistically described as an angel of apocalypse.

Part of the category mistake of paranoia and psychic channeling seems to come from a magnification of a marginal state of consciousness that we all have but tend to ignore in our modernist mentality. The Imagination has a fascinating ability to render unconscious sensing at the furthest periphery of mind into indirect communications. The invisible mites that live in our eyebrows or in the warp and woof of our bed linen have a curious way of showing up magnified as the bug-like monsters of our science fiction movies. In much the same way, bacteria can be turned into goblins, or the points of the crescent moon in juxtaposition to Mars can be seen as the claws of a witch about to scratch out the prince's eyes as he moves down below the horizon and disappears to wander in the wasteland before he reappears with Venus. We can also observe this process of imagistic transformation at work, if we examine our dreams and notice how a sound in the room will enter the narrative of our dreams, or how an infection will dramatize itself into the dream that precedes our becoming aware of the symptoms of the cold or flu. It is a common experience to have the image or voice of someone in our mind, and then the phone will ring, and it will be that person. If we were truly psychic, we would not need phones; but the interesting point is that although images and emotional feelings can be communicated, the conceptual, linguistic data of the message itself seems to require the telephone for its transmission.

A new form of scientific reductionism, one that has been popularized by Robert Ornstein and Julian Jaynes, would seek to explain all of the above experiences through the new variant of phrenology that is the theory of the lateralization of the brain. The Imagination is the ancient brain, a prelinguistic remnant of human evolution of 200,000 years ago when we had eyes to see and a nose to smell but lacked the appropriate jaw development for the rapid articulation of subtle linguistic sounds. As tongue and jaw developed with *Homo sapiens,* the older visual and olfactory ways of knowing were enveloped by new parts of the brain as the outer cortex began to supercede the limbic ring and a new hemispheric lateralization took over. Artists, psychics, shamans, and prophets are, therefore, from this neurological point of view, those who have the ancient physiology still dominant. They think in images, have visions and hear voices, and are not at home in the nonparticipatory mode of abstract conceptualization. And so to this day these evolutionary retards will have olfactory hallucinations, if they are schizophrenic, or if they are yogis in a Hindu culture, and are in the throes of the "elevation of kundalini," will experience the "siddhis" in which they smell auras and have intense color visions. The paranoids, those victims of a cultural evolution that has been accelerated by the electronic media, are those who suffer from the strictures and constrictions of our modernist, linear, print mentality and seek to overcome the cognitive dissonance between the exclusions of print and the simultaneities of electronics, as well as the dissonance between the two hemispheres, by becoming fanatically linear and literal. Paradoxically, paranoids suffer from an information-overload at one level, and an informational paucity at another, for they lack the wisdom and knowledge, both the ideas and the data, with which to transform their hunches into coherent theories or works of art.

Such a physiological theory of development is, of course, itself too literal and linear, for the interesting aspect of the dreams of scientists turned into theories, or the inuitions of artists turned into poetry, music, and painting, is precisely the manner in which auditory, olfactory, and visual perceptions are *reworked* into the conceptual and analytical modes of inte-grative thought. Consciousness is not limited to a lobe or a neural location, and Varela certainly argues that the globality of the whole neural system, and indeed of the whole body, has to be taken into an account of perception and mind. The artist or the artistic scientist does seem to have an openness to think-ing in images, and this hieroglyphic mode of thought seems to have been pronounced in individuals such as Einstein and Tesla, but the mathematical and linguistic articulation of these visions requires much more than half a brain. Consequently, it won't do to regard mystics, bards, and paranoids, or half-crazy scientists like Descartes, Gödel, or Tesla, as evolutionary re-tards whose corpus callosum was not yet wired up to connect their cerebral hemispheres.

When one stops to reflect on the creative process in sci-ence, there does seem to be a mode of contemplation in which the discursive mind is released to allow the image to arise. The creative personality seems to be the secure one that does not always need to be in control and can surrender, without pro-fessional anxiety, analysis to reverie.

This imagistic mode that we call the Imagination does seem to involve a prelinguistic form of mind in which thought is developed through correspondences, homologies, and par-ticipations of identity. This is like that, so use this to solve the problem of that: use the serpent biting its tail to go back to the problem to formulate the benzene ring; look into the bubbles of your beer glass and think of a bubble chamber as a way of rendering the atomic particles perceptible. This mode of side-stepping a problem, this mode of paraduction (as opposed to deduction, induction, and abduction) is paradoxical because it is a voluntary way of surrendering to involuntary means of thought, of letting the mind wander to gather what associa-tions it may, through dream, reverie, or vision. The image that pops into mind is uncalled for, just as my image of Dis-ney's dwarves working in the mines was not a logical response to Margulis's lecture about bacteria, but if the image is to have relevance, then the unpacking of its implications leads us to new understandings of the nature of the original object of attention.

Now the epistemologically interesting point to all of this is that these involuntary associations that come out of the blue do seem to have a form of pattern-recognition to them, one that works more through systems of correspondences and shapes than logic; these correspondences and homeomorphs are not arbitrary but seem to operate with an expanded perception of the nature of identity that is beyond what we construe as logical identity. From the influence of technology and especially the technology of computers and computations, we have tried to construe the brain as an information-processing machine and the mind as a logical computation of abstract symbols, but Mind seems to be much larger than this. If the unconscious mind goes off on a search during a reverie, it just doesn't go off in any direction, and what it brings forth is not often recognized as relevant or of value by those operating with too tight a logical definition of identity. It takes a more poetic and open kind of scientist to realize that a serpent biting its tail may be just what the conscious mind ordered when the unconscious mind went off on its reverie. There is a mind at work here, but it is not the kind of mind that we have been taught to respect in school.

If Mind is more than a tight rationality locked up in an ego that is "simply located" in an information-processing brain, then all this darkness we associate with the *ir*rational or the *un*conscious is simply our *in*ability to conceive of the other dimensional extensions of Mind as "the organization of the living." If we begin to appreciate that Mind is not simply located in three dimensions or four, then consciousness begins to take on a new shape, or a new topology. Mind, as Bateson proposed, extends beyond the pathways inside the body, and this larger Mind knows much and has its way of knowing and learning. So, when we decide to resolve a problem by "sleeping on it," we recognize that there are modes of accessing insights and ideas that are enhanced by "not thinking about it." When we sense or intuit or pick up (and notice how all our metaphors for these modes of knowing are limited by the physical senses) we are still unconscious of the material, so the imagination reworks it into the imagery of our habitual "world," and then we reprocess it once more into the socially approved rationality of our institutional world: depending on whether we are a priest in a temple, an artist in a studio, or a scientist in a laboratory. The Imagination is, therefore, precisely this sensitivity to the other dimensions of Mind. If in the medieval Cabbala or in modern String Theory in physics there are ten dimensions, the Imagination is the sensitivity that reconstitutes the inconceivable into the perceivable; and for this stepping down of ten dimensions into three, the physical body is both membrane and metaphor.[22]

If Mind is not simply located in a discrete ego, then, perhaps it is more appropriate to think of ourselves as a process, as one of Prigogine's dissipative structures rather than as a box of processed information. If Mind is immanent in the pathways that couple the organism to its environment, then there is a background mind that is prescient and extended.

Just as the cytoplasm surrounds the nucleus and through its complex enzymatic actions conditions the sequences and folding of the strands of DNA, so this extended mind surrounds the discrete, nucleated brain. To become aware of this background consciousness with its dimensional complexity can be called remembering, the *anamnesis* of Plato, or *samadhi* in a yogic form of practice that makes us aware that our location in a time- and space-bound world is merely a convenient framing that has become a habit. As I think and write I do not need to think of the individual muscular actions that allow me to touch the letters on the keyboard; so from infancy have we trained ourselves to shut out information so that we can operate

---

22 See Mark Johnson, *The Body in the Mind: The Bodily Basis of Meaning, Imagination and Reason* (Chicago: The University of Chicago Press, 1987).

quickly within the consensual domain of our inherited world. To go against the grain of this habitual world and to become conscious of the background mind that envelops us in its dimensional complexity takes a kind of meditational practice that only a yogi, an artist, or a contemplative scientist would endure. If we watch our mind falling asleep and develop a background consciousness to watching all our dreams, we can observe a watcher watching the ego watching its dreams. In this kind of mindfulness, "self" is no longer what we took it to be in the nucleated, corpuscular world of the ego in its habitual world.

Mind is indeed larger than ideologies or world views and as we become sensitive to multidimensionality at the edge of our limited forms of perception, we may register the images that are metaphors for the knowledge that is coming to us from all the other dimensions beyond the three we have habitually constituted as our "world." So we will envision the goblins and fairies that we cannot see. The image is, of course, only another form of conventionality, for if we put eagle's wings on human bodies to picture angels, we are simply suggesting that these topologically complex creatures are not limited to motion in two or three dimensions. The fundamentalist, unfortunately, cannot follow the symbolic utterance of the mystic and takes the image literally to think that angels really do have eagle's wings stuck onto their human backs. The mystic, endowed with an Imagination that is conscious in more than three dimensions, can see how an angel or fairy can be immanental in our world as viruses and bacteria, but can still extend to other modalities of worlds of light, vibration, music, and Mind.

If we come to the edge of our knowing, we have to imagine, and this horizontal world of myth cannot be understood as simply a world of deception and fantasy. The Imagination is like a transformer that takes electricity and steps it down to household current so that it can be used to run the appliances of our daily lives. And here I am using a metaphor to describe the metaphoric process through which the Imagination takes in knowledge and steps it down into the conventional imagery of the sensory world with which we are familiar. Mystical knowledge, achieved through meditation, can sensitize us to consciousness without a sensory percept or a conceptual syntax, and this is traditionally called consciousness without an object, or *samadhi,* but the Imagination is an intermediate realm, the realm of the artist, scientist, or prophet who renders the Intelligible into the Sensible.

In the prehistoric mentality expressed in the fairy tale, "Rapunzel," we saw patterns of correspondence between plants and planets, between pistils with collecting hairs and maidens in towers. For the pre-Copernican astronomy there is not a linearity of perspective in which the earth is foreground and the sun is background, or in which the perceiving subject is separated from an objective nature; rather, there is the form of prehistoric participation that Owen Barfield has discussed in which identity is shared between subject and object, between unique and universal.[23] Gaia as an evolutionary theory gives us a new way of appreciating how the part participates in the whole, but to appreciate the meta-dynamic by which an emergent phenomenon such as Gaia can learn and govern its autonomy as a planetary unity, we have to have a new understanding of cognitive biology. We have to move from the prehistoric participation of the ancient mentality, through the European modernist mentality with its linear system of perspective and its linear system of logic, fixed identity, and information-processing, to a new planetary mentality in which a posthistoric participation, or what Barfield called "Final Participation," is the mesocosm that connects the microcosm of the bacterial bioplasm to the macrocosm of the atmosphere.

It is, unfortunately, not the academic philosophers who are advancing this new planetary mentality. Academic philoso-

---

[23] See Owen Barfield, *Saving the Appearances* (New York: Harcourt Brace, 1972).

phy, like nineteenth-century philology before the emergence of linguistics or Renaissance theology before the emergence of modern science, is a finished and exhausted gold mine,[24] and it is now taking greater and greater applications of acids and caustics to force out the few remaining veins of worth. The environmental cost is too high to sustain this enterprise, so it is not surprising that the most valuable form of philosophy is no longer being done by professional academic philosophers.

Piaget read his Kant, took it seriously, and decided to see what was innate and what was learned by studying the growth of the mind through clinical research with children. In much the same way, Humberto Maturana and Francisco Varela have sought to answer philosophical questions through a natural epistemology in which neurophysiology was returned to its home in biology. In the European modernist era academic disciplines were "fields"; they were clearly marked out pieces of turf that were fiercely defended by alpha males in a hierarchical system of dominance. Philosophy was the most archetypally Germanic and authoritarian example of this mentality, and, I am afraid, still is. Contemporary cognitive science, however, is not a field, but an ecology of deserts and marshes. There is, of course, conflict and disagreement, but like the relationship between the ocean and the continent that drives the gaseous clouds of rain that are neither sea nor land but both, the relationship of opposition, say between electronic Artificial Intelligence and neurophysiology, or between cognitivism and connectionism, is a creative one in which even the thunderstorms charge the soil with the nitrogen the next generation requires.

---

[24] For me, Richard Rorty's *Philosophy and the Mirror of Nature* (Princeton, N.J.: Princeton University Press, 1979), like Robert Morley's last madrigal, sounds like a swan song.

CHAPTER THREE

INTELLECTUAL DOMINIONS AND COGNITIVE DOMAINS

1. THE LIFE OF DEATH IN THE WORK OF SCIENCE

PERHAPS IT IS GOING ON NOW. OR PERHAPS IT WILL not take place until we are into that last decade of this finishing millennium of Western Civilization. But soon, I believe, two vast empires of scientific research, fields that are now quite separated in different schools and buildings in our universities, will cross, and in their crossing breed a whole new culture in which "nature" as we have known it in preindustrial and industrial society will vanish. It will not be a culture that the cultured will recognize and accept. Indeed, it will be so unnatural that many may wish to call it inhuman and evil. And in their own way, they will be right, for the world it will bring forth will certainly be posthuman. The two empires of research that I have in mind are those of AIDS research and Artificial Intelligence.

Very soon all that we have learned about the immune system will be used in designing the architecture of Fifth- (even

Sixth-) Generation Computers, computers that can "think" and be self-programming. When carbon-based life and amorphous crystals are stitched together by the controlled "infection" of genetically engineered viruses, then all that we have learned from "fighting" AIDS will be shifted into a new context of designing loose plasmas of gnostic cells far more sophisticated than the rigid and linear suburban American lattices we call silicon chips. Just as Tokyo, as a gigantic protistic cell of a city, is far more complex in its ethnic homogeneity than the multiracial but linear grid of Los Angeles, so will these new planetary networks of living computers be far more sophisticated than our present binary engines with their dyadic logic of 1 and 0. With a modal logic of multiple dimensions flowing in a turbulence of creative noise in the chaos dynamics of a gnostic bioplasm, the spirit will at last be freed from the split between mind and matter. Mind will no longer be a subject *figured* against the *ground* of matter in the visual syntax of linear perspective; and as this *ground* dissolves it will take "nature" along with it. And when that happens, if it hasn't happened already in some government laboratory somewhere, our romantic and moralistic split between nature and culture will be dissolved as a Luciferic science weds itself to an Ahrimanic technology.[1] Curiously enough, this change of mind in rather introverted laboratories will be occurring in synchronous emergence with the outer transformation of humanity's adaptive niche in the biosphere as both the ozone hole and the greenhouse effect wear out the membrane between the atmosphere and the exhausted remains of our industrial society.

In other words, what we now experience as the plagues of AIDS and pollution may be part of an evolutionary conversation with the human species about the architecture of life and death, a conversation with a question as to where the identity of the living system is to be located in the emerging planetary

---

[1] For an explication of this mythological system, see Rudolph Steiner, *Lucifer and Ahriman* (London: Steiner Press, 1954).

bioplasm of this posthuman culture. We, with our European Enlightenment values of the individual and private property, locate identity in a "self." We envision this self, not as the chaotic dynamic of a nebular swirl, but as a container that holds identity and property through a system of ownership and rights. In our patriarchal imagination of what Laurie Anderson has called Big Science, we see the world as a collection of discrete individuals that own collectible things: egos contained in cars, wives, and paintings contained in houses, and kids contained in schools. But this new evolutionary conversation is questioning this Western way of constituting a world. The chaotic and polluted biosphere, the viral messengers transporting genes, the planetary bacterial bioplasms, they all seem to be suggesting to us, through the most basic characteristic of individuality, Death itself, that this vision of life in containers is not open enough for evolution. We are being asked to move out of our containers to enter into the evolutionary conversation to understand the biosphere and the emerging planetary culture as one in which Mankind (and I use the sexist term on purpose) as a defensive collection of competing and warring selves has come to its end.

The plague of AIDS now threatens us from within. Thermonuclear war threatens us from without. But from the very beginnings of immunology during the First World War, that old army doctor, Paul Ehrlich, sought to fight the infections of the wounded soldiers by marshaling the troops of the antibodies.[2] Even today at Ciba-Geigy's displays of the immune system for scientific expositions in Switzerland, the immune system is still presented in the terms of military defense. How we do delight in envisioning the antibodies as secret agents that circulate within the bloodstream and selectively take out those hidden subversives and aliens that cloak themselves in false identities and threaten the private property of the self.

---

[2] Remarks made by Francisco Varela in an address to the faculty and graduate student retreat of the Swiss Federal Institute of Technology of Zürich in Perugia, Italy, April 12, 1988.

And with another immune system raised on high into outer space through Star Wars, Big Science seeks to protect our body-politic with sensors and lasers that can take out the alien missiles as they violate the space that contains our nationalistic identity. What joins the empire of AIDS research to that of Star Wars is the field of electronics and the American, Manhattan Project way of doing research. In this male world of athletic science there is a strongly capitalistic competition and a Super Bowl, with its face-offs between the National Institutes of Health in Bethesda, Maryland, and the Pasteur Institute in Paris, or between the Silicon Valley and Tokyo.

There is one person who is already at work in these two areas of immunology and cognitive science, but his way of working and thinking in his tiny lab in Paris is almost the opposite of American Big Science. That person is, of course, Francisco Varela. Were I to give in to the American cultural addiction to hype, I would try to hold your attention by hailing him as "the Einstein of the Consciousness Movement,"[3] but this cultural mode of being able to feel hope only when one is pumped up with hype is precisely not the kind of philosophy that is expressed in Varela's subtle and slowly cumulative life's work. The new cultural imagination is not being brought down from the mountain top by some single solitary genius, be he a Moses or an Einstein; it is being brought forth in concert with others in a global state that emerges from the play of a distributive lattice. What Abraham, Lovelock, Margulis, and Varela have in common is that they are all marginal figures to the world of Big Science. Abraham is at Santa Cruz, not Berkeley; Lovelock is a solitary eccentric in a mill in Devon, not in a lab at Cambridge; Margulis is at the University of Massachusetts, not Harvard; and Varela is at Paris VI, and not MIT. The kind of science they do is profoundly related to the way they do it. "Small is beautiful"

---

[3] A phrase that has been already used by a journalist to describe Ken Wilber; characteristically, the blurb is to be found on the back of all Wilber's books.

can be as true of science as of economics, for as Lovelock likes to jest in all seriousness with "Lovelock's Law," there is often an inverse relationship between Cost and Worth. On this human scale of doing science as if people mattered, there is certainly no bitter gulf separating the sciences from the humanities. If we were to follow this way of knowing, perhaps, the Luciferic inflation of genetic engineering and the Ahrimanic collectivation of technicians in the laboratories of the military-industrial state could be avoided. Chaos dynamics teaches us about the cumulative effect of small changes, so the heroic mode of the Big Science of competing super powers may be just that kind of nationalistic activity that is no longer appropriate to the emergence of a new planetary culture.

Neither Lovelock, Margulis, nor Varela would choose to express themselves in the futuristic and science fiction mode that I have adopted here momentarily to imagine the implications of the present, but they would all be able to listen and hear, for their way of working does not isolate them into specialized hit squads within imperial forces. Varela may not express himself in the mythic language of Lovelock, or the geometrical hieroglyphs of Abraham, but he does choose a distinctly evocative language that speaks of "autopoiesis" and "the bringing forth of worlds." And almost alone among biologists he does recognize that the time has come to build a bridge between immunology and cognitive science.

There is a strong intuitive sense in which immune systems are cognitive: they recognize molecular shapes, remember the history of encounters of an individual organism, define the boundaries of a molecular "self," and make inferences about molecular species likely to be encountered. By and large immunology has left these admittedly cognitive terms undefined or at a metaphorical level and has concentrated, instead, on the molecular details of immune components. The first intention of this paper is to argue that by so doing one is leaving unexamined and shrouded in a fog of mystery the most interesting domain of phenomena the immune systems affords to animals: their cognitive abilities. To advance in this direction, one must be willing to embark on an explicit examination of the cognitive mechanisms proper to the immune system.[4]

Consistent with his Buddhist orientation to the philosophy of life, Varela questions the whole militaristic way of envisioning the immune system:

> We must replace the notion of the lymphoid system as a collection of unconnected lymphocyte clones carrying receptors directed outward (toward unpredictable encounters with foreign materials), with the notion of a network of interacting lymphocytes, where the receptors are directed inward, making the activities of the whole lymphoid system curl and close onto itself. . . . We don't "turn on" the lymphoid system of an animal when we expose it to an antigen; the lymphocytes are already operating before we intervene.[5]

From Varela's point of view as a Chilean alien in the world of Gringo Science, the immune system is a linguistic domain that is in communication with itself, and in this ongoing conversation, aliens are not invaders, for we are always awash with aliens, they simply are entities that are not engaged in speaking the same language. Lewis Thomas, following up on some of Lynn Margulis's work that has shown how "invading" microbes can become endosymbionts,[6] has reported on work that has shown that if a neonate mouse is infected with men-

---

[4] Francisco J. Varela, Antonio Coutinho, Bruno Dupire, and Nelson N. Vaz, "Cognitive Networks: Immune, Neural, and Otherwise" in *Theoretical Immunology*, Santa Fe Institute in the Sciences of Complexity, Ed., A. S. Perelson (Boston: Addison-Wesley, 1988), p. 1.

[5] Francisco J. Varela, *Principles of Biological Autonomy*, (New York: Elsevier North Holland, 1979), pp. 216–217.

[6] See Lynn Margulis, "Genetic and Evolutionary Consequences of Symbiosis: A Review," *Experimental Parasitology*, Vol. 39, 277–349 (1976); p. 310. See also Lewis Thomas, "At the Mercy of Our Defenses" in *Earth's Answer*, Eds., Katz, Marsh, and Thompson (New York, Harper & Row, 1977), pp. 156–169. The militaristic way of looking at the immune system was first challenged by the brilliant Polish-Israeli scientist, Ludwik Fleck; see his *Genesis and Development of a Scientific Fact* (Chicago: Basel, 1935; University of Chicago Press, 1979), p. 59.

ingitis, it dies, for its immune system reads the presence as a threat; but if a mouse foetus is infected, it does not read the presence as a threat, sees the invader as part of itself, tolerates it, and by not marshaling its defense system, does not kill itself. And oh what a powerful metaphor lies within this narrative of Big Science, aliens, and national defense industries.

> Thus the central distinction in the operation of the lymphoid system is not between "self" and "nonself," but rather between what can and what cannot interact with the immunological structure: a distinction between identity and "nonsense," or immunological "noise."[7]

From a cultural-historical point of view this philosophy of the immune system of Varela is no longer within the mentality of modernism with its narratives of linear perspective and linear causation, and so it is not surprising that it has required a different philosophy and a more open cultural space in which to grow and develop. In modernism the ruling idea is one of a template receiving impressions. One kind of impact on a template gives us ideas, another gives us a painting on a canvas, and another gives us a disease; thus epistemology, aesthetics, and medicine all have in common a similar way of looking at the world.

The rise of modernism saw the emergence of a new relationship between art and science in the Italian Renaissance, for as both Heisenberg and Whitehead have pointed out, the close analysis of nature in painting preceded the rise of scientific empiricism by over a century. As painting began to become secularized in its depiction of landscapes that were not stages for religious events, the representation of nature began to be an idea that was developed by both art and science. With the rise of perspective in Alberti and Brunelleschi, and the invention of the *camera oscura,* the brain began to be seen as a

---

[7] Varela, *Principles of Biological Autonomy*, p. 219.

box that was taking in light and information from the outside world and creating an internal representation of the larger world. For both literature and art, *mimesis* was the mode of human creativity. This is the mentality of modernism, and it is a cultural mode of the imagination that embraces both art and science, for one cannot talk about the scientific examination of nature and ignore Bellini, da Vinci, and Dürer, and one cannot talk about the perception of light in seventeenth-century thought and speak only of Hüyghens and not of Van Ruysdael and Rembrandt. The physics of objects in space for Galileo and Newton is also the space for the setting up of an observer in the mode of linear perspective articulated by Alberti and Brunelleschi, and with the notion of perspective one encounters the construction of a linear space in which the object is objective and the perceptions are subjective, for each painter will see the landscape in a slightly different light. This split world ruled until the time when the atom began to be split, for then from the impact of quantum mechanics and expressionism, the observer began to take on a different phenomenology. It is with the naive idea of the dominant power of a scientifically objective observer that the Chilean biologists, Francisco Varela and his teacher Humberto Maturana, part company with their Anglo-American colleagues.[8]

Precisely because the imagination is a transformer that is a living membrane between the unknown and the known, it is a mode of sensitivity that lives between the cultural unconscious and the accepted societal modes of expression. When the conventional mode of imagining the world in medievalism began to be abandoned by artists and scientists in the Renaissance, it was not simply the case of a mass of new facts coming in; it was an entirely new mentality, a new mode of imagining.

---

[8] See Humberto Maturana, "Everything Said Is Said by an Observer" in *Gaia, A Way of Knowing: The Political Implications of the New Biology*, Ed., W. I. Thompson (Great Barrington, Mass.: Lindisfarne Press, 1987), pp. 65–82. See also Humberto Maturana and Francisco Varela, *The Tree of Knowledge* (Boston: New Science Library, 1987), p. 27.

What is most startling about these periods of cultural shift is that they behave much more like an undirected ecology of mind than a directed ideology conducted by a leader. There is no Lenin at the Finland Station for the Renaissance. There is, in the language of Ludwik Fleck, a "thought style" and a "thought collective"[9] in which groups of artists and scientists will *feel* more in harmony with some thinkers than others. In the formative stages of the emergence of a thought collective, the emergent properties can be unconscious and synchronous. Just as there was a synchronous relationship in the emergence of *mimesis* in art and the representation of nature in modernist science, so is there now a synchronous emergence in the shift from *mimesis* to *fabrication* in our electronic culture and our electronic world economy. And just as there was the *camera oscura* for *mimesis,* so is there now the video-synthesizer for the new mentality in which what you see in a video is not a copy of "the outside world" but a complete fabrication of reality. And as it was once before in the Italian Renaissance, so is it now in the planetary renaissance in which the electronic video artists and the informational *Wissenskünstler* are at work alongside the scientists. In this moment from the nihilism of postmodernism to the imaginative creativity of planetary culture, the old divisions between the objective sciences and the subjective arts, the "Two Cultures" of C. P. Snow, are transcended.[10]

Ludwik Fleck's observations on the effect of thought collectives in the development of scientific facts came about through his study of the historical development of the understanding and treatment of syphilis. From the medieval notion of this plague as the Last Judgment of God, to the seventeenth century "French Pox" that could be blamed on unclean and sexually overactive animalistic aliens, to the spirochete re-

---

[9] Ludwik Fleck, *The Genesis and Development of a Scientific Fact,* p. 38.

[10] See *IS Journal* 1 (Los Angeles: December, 1986), in passim. Gene Youngblood and Bill Viola are two video artists who have been particularly influenced by the work of Maturana and Varela.

vealed by the microscope and Wassermann Test, the cultural history of syphilis is also the cultural history of the development of the mentality of modernism. There seems to be a cultural pathology to diseases that makes them part of a larger civilizational phenomenology, and not simply a chance infection. The shift from medievalism to modernism pivots around the year 1500, and it was slightly before this time, in 1486, that the artist Hieronymus Bosch was at work painting his visions of the end of the world in "The Last Judgment." It was not the end of the world, but it was the end of a world-system. The world ecclesia was replaced by a world economy, and part of the trade between the old world and the new was not simply in gold. Crops like corn, tobacco, chocolate, tomatoes, and potatoes were brought to Europe, and horses, cereals, and livestock were brought to America. Along with this exchange of visible ecologies, there was also an exchange of the invisible ecosystems of microbes: Europe exported small pox and imported syphilis. The changing narratives for the phenomenology of syphilis, therefore, also narrate the cultural history of Europe in its development of the new world economy with its related mentality of modernism.

And so it is with our contemporary plague of AIDS. The narratives that we put forth are mythopoeic constructions. First we had a myth of hominization and origins and saw the disease as coming from darkest Africa. Then we saw it as a new kind of "French Pox" that we could blame on those disgustingly sexually overactive aliens, the homosexuals, who brought it in from Africa by having unnatural sex with boys in Haiti. Then we thought that we had isolated a causal agent in the HIV virus and began to marshall the massive funding needed to create a powerful drug with which we could bomb the invading intraterrestrial. Now we begin to suspect that AIDS isn't a single infecting virus striking the template of the organism, but a whole ecology of diseases springing from the ecological disruption of membranes through deforestation in Africa, and the consequent encounter of humans and monkeys; and we are just beginning to wonder whether AIDS could also signify an even greater "membrane" anomaly that calls upon us to reconceptualize the "nature" of "the self." If, from the influence of a Varelan way of thinking, we begin to suspect that a pathogen isn't an object, but a relationship in a linguistic domain, then we may need to change our ideas of treatment to ones in which the immune system is "retuned" to new states of harmonic integration in which we learn to tolerate aliens by seeing the self as a cloud in a clouded sky and not as a lord in a walled-in fortress. Such medicine is more likely to be inexpensive and "alternative," and, therefore, not especially welcome in the seats of power in the Big Science world of the National Institutes of Health, the Pasteur Institute, or Merck and Ciba-Geigy.

2. PHILOSOPHY AND COGNITIVE SCIENCE

THE PLACE OF Paris in Varela's work may be no accidental location, for Paris has always been a city of philosophers, and may now be just the right place to achieve a position of balance between North American domination and Latin American subordination. Certainly, Paris has a rich tradition of research in the biological sciences, from Louis Pasteur to François Jacob. Moreover, Varela's decision to work in just those areas of research in immunology and cognitive science that are dominated by the colossal institutions of Big Science is clearly one way of confronting head-on the differences between Continental and Anglo-American ways of thinking.

"Thinking otherwise" could serve as a good subtitle for this book, for what is being expressed is precisely that kind of mystical fondness for the imagination that has no place in our departments of philosophy. For the Anglo-American world view, the building blocks of reality are objects, be they discrete subatomic particles, genes, or "agents of mind"; and perceptions are simply neurologically imperfect copies of these "things" that are "out there." The discovery of novelty is, therefore, never an entry into a new dimension or a new way of imagining the world; it is simply the addition of a smaller particle on which to base the entirety of the world picture. Marvin Minsky, one of the founding fathers of Artificial Intelligence at MIT, speaks very well for this Anglo-American tradition when he tells us that his new book "will show how the tiny machines that we'll call 'agents of mind' could be the long-sought 'particles' that those theories need."[11] For this straightforward and unambiguous world, first one has things, then one builds a world up with all the discrete little bits: the genes give one an organism, the agents give one a mind. Never mind that the genes in the cell depend upon thousands of other factors, from the topological folding of the strand of DNA to the concerted action of enzymes within the cytoplasm, and never mind that more efferent than afferent neurons unfold from the lattice of the brain so that the organism confronts its environment on its own terms; never mind, for this is a world view of matter and never of mind.

As the apologetics for a new ambitious, technocratic and global, managerial class, cognitive science is, in many ways, not unambiguously bad, for before the rise of cognitive science, philosophy was mired in the alluvium of the ebbing flood of modernism. The streams of the giants had receded and a lot of little fish in philosophy departments were left flopping on the strand or swimming, like leviathans in puddles, around in circles for the admiration of only those minnows who happened to be their graduate students.

The cultural difficulties arise when cognitive science simply projects the narrow ethnocentrisms of the North American world view. For the last three centuries there has been an Atlantic hobby-horse rocking back and forth between British Empiricism and Continental Rationalism. This oscillation has

---

[11] Marvin Minsky, *The Society of Mind* (New York: Simon & Schuster, 1986), p. 19.

continued all through our century, for one could escape the logical positivism of Ayer with the metalogical mysticism of Wittgenstein, the mechanistic psychology of Watson with the phenomenology of Merleau-Ponty, the behaviorism of Skinner with the Cartesian Linguistics of Chomsky or the Kantian genetic epistemology of Piaget.

The positive side to "the mind's new science" is that in extending philosophy into many disciplines, it has shown just how inadequate single disciplines are.[12] But if single disciplines are inadequate, how much the more so are single cultures, so the world view of MIT and Harvard begins to be too narrow for the construction of an entire philosophy of mind. Small wonder that one Latin American who contributed to the foundations of cognitive science, Humberto Maturana, chose to quit the capital of Cambridge, U.S.A., to return to his native Chile in pursuit of a form of natural epistemology that was not allowed in the Research Laboratory of Electronics at MIT during the late fifties.[13]

No scientific paper in cognitive science captures this historical period of transition from postwar to postindustrial as much as "What the Frog's Eye Tells the Frog's Brain," and no technical paper has had as much influence on the general culture, on art as well as philosophy, as this particular work.[14]

---

[12] For a very North American view of the history of cognitive science, see Howard Gardener's *The Mind's New Science* (New York: Basic Books, 1985).

[13] See Humberto Maturana's Introduction to *Autopoiesis and Cognition: The Realization of the Living*, H. R. Maturana and Francisco J. Varela (Boston: Reidel, 1980).

[14] For an illustration of the effect of this paper on the video artist Bill Viola, see "From Eisenstein to Einstein: The Video of Bill Viola, A Conversation with Bill Viola, David Dunn, and Allyn B. Brodsky," in *IS Journal* 11 (Los Angeles: December 1987), p. 69. See also the discussion in Nelson Goodman's *Ways of Worldmaking* (Indianapolis: Hackett, 1978), p. 73. For a much more exciting and philosophically rich contribution to the U.S.A.'s overcoming the split between British Empiricism and Continental Rationalism, see George Lakoff, *Women, Fire, and Dangerous Things* (Chicago: University of Chicago Press, 1987) and Mark Johnson, *The Body in the Mind: The Bodily Basis of Meaning, Imagination, and Reason* (Chicago: University of Chicago Press, 1987).

The conventional wisdom about perception at that time was that the eye was a lens that passed on information to the brain, so that it in its turn could sort out all the wave-lengths and intensities of light to come up with the familiar world of objects sitting colorfully in physical space. What Lettvin and Maturana discovered, however, was that "the eye speaks to the brain in a language already highly organized and interpreted, instead of transmitting some more or less accurate copy of the distribution of light on the receptors."[15] The conventional notion, derived from Lockian Empiricism, would have it that the intensity of light has an impact on the template of the retina, and this "impression" is transmitted to the brain for sorting and transformation into "ideas"; Lettvin and Maturana discovered that it was "not the light intensity itself but rather the *pattern* of local variation of intensity that is the exciting factor." In other words, there was a geometry of the perceptual mechanism that was constructing a world view in terms of symmetries, proportions, and ratios, and not simply in terms of impacts and intensities.

The "Frog's Eye" was written in 1959, and in 1960 Humberto Maturana returned to Chile. If the paper played down the notion of the simple impact of light on the nervous system, the paper itself had enormous impact, for the idea of a Research Laboratory of Electronics carrying out research in neurophysiology was charismatic and it excited science fiction visions, in the minds of people like Herman Kahn, of brains directly hooked up to computers for the achievement of higher intelligence. From José Delgado's proclamations about "The Physical Control of the Mind" to the recent cover of *BYTE*

---

[15] Warren McCulloch and Walter Pitts, as the senior scientists and founding fathers of the Research Laboratory of Electronics, were the secondary signatories to this famous paper, but the actual work was carried out by Lettvin and Maturana. See J. Y. Lettvin, H. K. Maturana, W. S. McCulloch, and W. H. Pitts, *Proceedings of the Institute of Radio Engineers*, Vol. 47 (New York, 1959), pp. 1940–1951. This paper is reprinted in Warren McCulloch's *Embodiments of Mind* (Cambridge, Mass.: MIT Press, 1965).

magazine, which shows a mouse neuron connected and interacting with a silicon computer chip, the entire relationship of nature and culture was beginning to be transformed.

For Maturana back in Chile the lessons to be learned from the paper were quite other than the ones being picked up on by the proponents of A.I. and the computer hackers. Along with thinkers such as Gregory Bateson, who in the 1960s was developing a philosophy of information based on pattern and difference and not impact as the trigger to changes of state, Maturana brooded on the implications of the primacy of pattern over substance,[16] and the more he thought about it, the more uncomfortable he became with the Anglo-American objectivist tradition.

> When Jerry Y. Lettvin and I wrote our several articles on frog vision . . . we did it with the implicit assumption that we were handling a clearly defined cognitive situation: there was an objective (absolute) reality, external to the animal, and independent of it (not determined by it), which it could perceive (cognize), and the animal could use the information obtained in its perception to compute a behavior adequate to the perceived situation. . . . But even there the epistemology that guided our thinking and writing was that of an objective reality independent of the observer.[17]

With sufficient distance in Santiago to look back on his work in Cambridge, Maturana began to part company with American Big Science to take a more European and

---

[16] Gregory Bateson participated in the Macy Conferences that helped to formulate the early version of the field of cybernetics, and Bateson, along with Heinz von Foerster and Humberto Maturana, took part in the Wenner-Gren Foundation conferences in the 1960s. For Bateson's thoughts on pattern, see his classic paper, "Form, Substance and Difference" in *Steps to an Ecology of Mind* (New York: Ballantine, 1972), pp. 448–466. In the 1970s and early 1980s, Bateson, Maturana, von Foerster, and Varela took part in the Lindisfarne conferences, and in the cases of Bateson and Varela, actually served as Lindisfarne Scholars-in-Residence.

[17] See Humberto Maturana's Introduction to Maturana and Varela's *Autopoiesis and Cognition: The Realization of the Living*, H.R. Maturana and Francisco J. Varela (Boston: Reidel 1980), p. xiv.

thoughtful approach in the formulation of a natural epistemology. "What if, instead of attempting to correlate the activity in the retina with the physical stimuli external to the
organism, we did otherwise, and tried to correlate the activity
in the retina with the color experience of the subject?"[18] As he
began to question and think otherwise, Maturana began to in-
cline toward the more continental, Kantian side of the great
cultural divide of the English Channel.

> In other words, the new approach required us to treat seriously
> the activity of the nervous system as determined by the nervous
> system itself, and not by the external world; thus the external
> world would only have a triggering role in the release of the
> internally-determined activity of the nervous system.[19]

What seemed to confirm Maturana in his studies of vision
was his moving from research on the configuration of vision in
frogs to the study of color vision in the primate retina.

> I soon realized in my research that my central purpose in the
> study of color vision could not be the study of a mapping of a
> colorful world on the nervous system, but rather that it had to
> be the understanding of the participation of the retina (or ner-
> vous system) in the generation of the color space of the ob-
> server.[20]

Dogs have two cones as photo receptors and thus have
two-dimensional color vision, the black and white world of
perception in full moonlight. Primates and humans have three
cones and thus have the world we know as colored, but birds
have four types of receptors, and therefore experience a
world we can only imagine,[21] so it makes little sense to think

---

[18] Ibid., p. xv.

[19] Ibid., p. xv.

[20] Ibid., p. xii.

[21] Since this is a work devoted to the imagination, I wish to propose my imagination of this cognitive domain that comes from my own experience of Goethean Science as "participation" with birds. One morning in June in Bern I was, as usual,
awakened by the songbirds at about 4:45. As it was too early to rise or go back to
sleep, I sat in meditation, listened to the song birds, and received the following in-

that there is one single and objective world in which we all live. "We do not see the 'space' of the world; we live our field of vision. We do not see the 'colors' of the world; we live our chromatic space."[22]

In research on the frog's eye, Maturana discovered the importance of patterns of light intensity and motion, but in the consideration of the color vision of primates he had to confront a situation in which perception was not simply a reporting on conditions in an objective world, but, rather, the carving out of a specific "cognitive domain." The external environment could, therefore, no longer remain as the determining space it had in the traditional Darwinian narratives with their emphasis on *adaptation;* in fact, the more Maturana considered it, the more the nervous system began to appear to him to be a closed network.

It was at this point in his work in Chile in the sixties that Maturana encountered his *wunderkind* pupil, Francisco Varela, a pupil who very quickly became a colleague. The story goes

---

sights. The fourth dimension of tetra-chromaticity is time and the birds are perceiving color as a tone that is a process and not an object defined in a figure-ground gestalt. We perceive a red flower against a green background, or an accelerating car in the street, and make judgments of when it is safe to cross. Birds, however, see two skies, or a sky behind our sky, and this is a horizonal event and not a targeted object figured against a ground. Birds use the oscillating tone, like the crystal in our quartz watches, the pulse going back and forth between the two skies, as a way of telling time with the incredible precision that allows them to know when to start singing, or when to leave in their migrations. Humans see the colors of dawn only as *finished* events, as time as it is expressed in the perfective aspect of Greek or Russian grammar: it is black outside, or pearl gray, or blue; but birds are perceiving the temporal relationship of color tones as they are going on. Color is music to their eyes. Appropriately enough, considering their sensitivity, their songs at dawn and dusk are quite different, and quite musically complex, so this musical sensitivity brings forth a sensitivity to time that enables them to perceive color tones, in synaesthesia, as temporal events, analogous to our perception of the acceleration of an object as a temporal-spatial event. What this means as guidelines for future research is that birds should not be studied merely in a laboratory with discrete lights and discrete objects, but they should be studied in natural habitats or on the top of university buildings where their horizonal discrimination of the two skies, of the sky behind the sky, can be performed and observed by humans.

[22] Maturana and Varela, *The Tree of Knowledge,* p. 23.

that one day an eager and enthusiastic undergraduate appeared in Professor Maturana's office and announced that he had come to see him because he wanted "to study the role of Mind in the Universe." Having done enough research on eyes and vision, Maturana seemed to like what he saw in this nineteen-year-old's field of vision, for he responded to his lack of social sophistication with a whimsical smile of approval and said: "My boy, you've come to the right place."

But even at age nineteen, Varela was no philosophical innocent. As a high school student at the German Lyceum in Santiago, he had been trained by German Jesuits and had read Heidegger's *Sein und Zeit* in the original before he had even begun his undergraduate studies in biology. Just as Piaget had studied Kant and decided to study the construction of reality in the perceptions of children as a way of answering some philosophical questions through clinical research rather than textual analysis, so did Varela move into neurophysiology from phenomenology as his own way of questioning the text of Being of the philosopher in the context of the study of living beings.

It did not take Varela much time to come out of the Heideggerian *holzwege* to the horizon of the unknown. He entered the University of Chile in 1965, but by 1968 he was following in Maturana's footsteps and going off to get his doctorate at Harvard. Two years later, at the age of twenty-three, he had his Ph.D. in hand and had written his thesis on "Insect Retinas: Information processing in the compound eye."

Varela returned to Chile in 1970, so he had the time and space to put his experience in the intellectual capital of the American Empire into a more global perspective. Once he was back on his native ground and working again with Maturana, their more continental approach began to distance itself from the information-processing orientation of the American engineers.

In writing the 1980 introduction to his 1970 paper "Biol-

ogy of Cognition," Maturana felt uncomfortable with the fact
that he had given in to pressures from his colleagues to construe the external environment as the causal force that im-
pacted on the template of the organism. Two years later in
1972, through collaboration with Varela, he broke out of this
"allopoetic mode" of imagining the relationship of the organism to the environment and developed the idea of "autopoiesis" as a narrative in which to re-envision the dynamics of
life. If the nervous system was closed and the organism encountered the environment on its own terms, then the organism was not "adapting" to an external world, but was moving
through time in a process of "natural drift" in which its structure was being conserved. This conservation of structure
could be called "adaptation," just as long as one did not con-
fuse the domains of discourse, of the organism and the observer. This confusion was, of course, precisely what his
colleagues did make, and so Maturana and Varela definitely
broke ranks in the formulation of their theory of "Autopoiesis
and Cognition":

> I made a concession which I have always regretted. I submitted
> to the pressure of my friends and talked about causal relations
> when speaking about the circular organization of living sys-
> tems. To do this was both inadequate and misleading. It was
> inadequate because the notion of causality is a notion that per-
> tains to the domain of descriptions, and as such it is relevant
> only in the metadomain in which the observer makes his com-
> mentaries and cannot be deemed to be operative in the phe-
> nomenal domain, the object of the description.[23]

In articulating the concept of autopoiesis, Maturana and
Varela helped to resolve a long-standing problem with the definition of life in biology. Everyone knew what life was, but the
best that the biologists could come up with was a list of items
like reproduction, irritability, and motion. The problem was
that the definition invoked what it tried to explain and that

---

[23] Maturana and Varela, *Autopoiesis and Cognition*, p. xviii.

107

the list had no particular sense of the morphology of living behavior, the virtual organization of the living. An automobile has motion, but it does not produce its own components, for they are allopoetically produced in a factory; the living cell, however, does produce its own components, and does maintain this structural organization of process through time, and when it ceases, it is no longer a question of life, but of death.[24]

With the articulation of the idea of autopoiesis, the natural epistemology of Maturana and Varela began to pick up speed and the distance between it and the conventional wisdom of the cognitive science of Cambridge, U.S.A., began to be truly vast. Cognition, rather than being seen as epiphenomenal to an organism's strategy of adaptation, now began to be seen by them as fundamentally "the organization of the living." This was so profound and radical a departure in the philosophy of biology that even today few of their North American colleagues can appreciate this intellectual revolution that has been effected without them. And revolution it literally was, for Maturana and Varela, in their articulation of autopoiesis, were turning things upside down to take cognition all the way down to the cellular level. Intuiting that this mode of description opened up new ways of looking at the problems of cognition and re-cognition, Varela expanded his research from vision in the retina to re-cognition in the immune system.[25]

Maturana and Varela's next step in their formulation of this new field of cognitive biology was even more radical, and is, perhaps, the reason why it is still hard for their colleagues with an engineering approach to "information-processing" to follow them. Precisely because they were aliens and not native

---

[24] See Francisco J. Varela, *Principles of Biological Autonomy* (New York: Elsevier Holland, 1979), p. 13.

[25] See N. Vaz, and F. Varela, "Self and Non-sense: An Organism-Centered Approach to Immunology" in *Medical Hypothesis*, 1978, 4:231–267. See also F. Varela, "The Immune Network: Self and Non-sense in the Molecular Domain" in *Principles of Biological Autonomy*.

to the Anglo-American traditions of objectivism, but were Chileans raised with an orientation to Europe, they were able to take a radical step that was literally inconceivable in either of the Cambridges: they threw out the whole notion of "representation" in describing the biological roots of knowing the world.

Now it is almost an article of faith as articulated by the orthodox priests of North American cognitive science, men like Fodor and Pylyshyn, that there can be "no computation without representation."

> One of the central proposals that I examine is the thesis that what makes it possible for humans (and other members of the natural kind informavore) to act on the basis of representations is that they instantiate such representations physically as cognitive codes and that their behavior is a causal consequence of operations carried out on these codes. Since this is precisely what computers do, my proposal amounts to a claim that cognition is a type of computation.[26]

The difficulty in assessing the nature of the disagreements between the cognitivists and the Santiago school is that the MIT people seem to be trying to get at the *preconditions* for thought and are not so much talking about cognition as precognition; they are, in fact, articulating a new kind of intellectual unconscious. The relationship of this intellectual unconscious to conscious thought is, therefore, homeomorphic to other recent attempts to excavate consciousness. What Lévy-Straus's structuralist *mythologique* is to a concrete, Amazonian mythological narrative, or what Foucault's *episteme* is to a seventeenth-century field of knowledge, or what a sociobiologist's calculus of inclusive fitness and the gene pool is for an animal selecting a mate, seem all to be homeomorphic to what Fodor and Pylyshyn have in mind when they take cog-

---

[26] Zenon W. Pylyshyn, *Computation and Cognition: Toward a Foundation for Cognitive Science* (Cambridge, Mass.: MIT Press, 1984), p. xiii. See also Jerry Fodor, *The Language of Thought* (Cambridge, Mass.: Harvard University Press, 1975).

nition to be a type of computation, a processing of abstract symbols that generates observed behavior. The excavation of an intellectual unconscious (as opposed to the instinctive unconscious of Freud or the collective unconscious of Jung) would seem to be, therefore, one of the major developments of thought since the nineteen sixties. This precognitive operation of symbols, information-processing, and consequent mapping of an objective, external world is not, however, what Maturana and Varela have in mind when they speak of cognition as "the organization of the living." Indeed, one of the reasons why we seem to be proliferating so many different kinds of the unconscious, from Freud to Jung to Lévy-Strauss and Foucault to Fodor and Pylyshyn, is precisely because our notion of mind is so inadequate that we continually have to shore it up with an unconscious that is the basin for everything we can't explain when we insist on regarding mind as epiphenomenal and unreal. Perhaps if we truly began to appreciate the *nature* of Mind as "the organization of the living" in the ways that Maturana and Varela suggest, we could begin to achieve an intellectual coherence for cognitive biology that would be, literally, a philosophy of Life.

For North American cognitive science, however, this paradigm shift is far off, and only a few cognitive scientists such as Winnograd, Flores, Lakoff, and Johnson have begun to break ranks. Indeed, the defection of Terry Winnograd from MIT is seen by Marvin Minsky as nothing less than a heretical fall from the true faith; so, clearly, more heresy trials and inquisitions are waiting for those untenured professors who refuse to contribute to the illusions of Artificial Intelligence that draw forth such vast sums from governments and multinational corporations. At the present moment, there is no question but that the brain is an information-processing device, and that the way this information is processed is through the computational manipulation of symbols that map onto an external world and enable the organism to fit into the constraints of his environment. Anything else is unthinkable, and in a recent scientific conference at Stanford, Jerome Feldman of Rochester and Gunther Stent of Berkeley did not simply disagree with Varela, they recited the Catechism of Cognitivism, entoned "No computation without representation" and insisted that there wasn't anything to talk about. Not only was Varela not in their school, he was not even in their culture.

When I as a student of cultural history sit in an audience and observe this sort of collision between what Ludwik Fleck called "thought styles" and "thought collectives," I know that I am watching something larger than a mere clash of opinions. I am observing the clash of two historical mentalities and no piling up of data will ever convince anyone to change one's mind. One can change one's mind with facts, but to change mentalities one has to change the structure of one's world view and one's cultural process of identification with favored groups and their value systems. This metanoia is so close to a death experience that people who survive it often do so through a sickness unto death or a conversion experience in which the personality is radically transformed. Most people would rather die than go through that agony of loss, and so the usual way in which a cultural shift is effected is through the death of the Establishment. The Princes of the Church do not convert to becoming followers of Galileo; they simply die and a new generation comes along with a different historical orientation.

And so it is today, for the population biologists cannot accept the Gaia hypothesis of Lovelock and Margulis, for they require abandonment of their central tenet: that evolution is the work of male organisms in competition to leave more offspring, as well as admission of the existence of the connection between atmospheric chemistry and metabolism. The climatologists and geophysicists, however, are looking at precisely those forms of planetary metabolism in which the geophysiology of the Gaia hypothesis begins to make sense, and they know how to conceive of tests in which to study the relations of the life in the ocean and the atmospheric stabilization of the global climate. And it is much the same disciplinary condition with natural epistemology, for the leaders in Artificial Intelligence are hardly the ones who are going to be taken with the work of Maturana and Varela, for their funding depends on convincing governments that they can compete with Japan to come up with Fifth Generation computers on which the national economy and the national defense depend. The kind of thinkers who are attracted to the cognitive biology of Maturana and Varela are general systems theorists such as Erich Jantsch,[27] atmospheric chemists such as Lovelock, biologists such as Margulis, California computer scientists such as Winnograd and Flores,[28] artists such as Youngblood and Viola, and futurists such as Peter Schwartz and Hazel Henderson.

The loss of the notion of representation leads ultimately to the loss of the idea of a fixed ground to an objective, independent reality, and Varela has not backed away from the implications of his own work, but has begun, in collaboration with other students of Buddhist philosophy and cognitive science, to explore the imaginary landscapes of just such "Worlds Without Ground."[29] This world view of groundlessness appears to be the dividing point between a literate and an electronic culture, for the loss of faith in representation upsets the Reformation-based culture, one that requires the fixed text of the Bible for religion and the fixed text of nature for science, but it does not unsettle the post-sixties generation, for you

---

[27] See Erich Jantsch, *The Self-Organizing Universe* (Oxford: Pergamon Press, 1980).

[28] See Terry Winnograd and Fernando Flores, *Understanding Computers and Cognition: A New Foundation for Design* (Norwood, N.J.: Ablex Press, 1986).

[29] See *Worlds Without Ground*, work in progress, Francisco Varela and Evan Thompson, scheduled for publication in 1990. An excellent work that has already appeared in the field of cognitive science, one that is critical of the objectivist tradition in philosophy and takes a point of view that is harmonic with the enactive cognitive science of Varela, is Mark Johnson's *The Body in the Mind: The Bodily Basis of Meaning, Imagination, and Reason* (Chicago: University of Chicago Press, 1987). See also George Lakoff, *Women, Fire, and Dangerous Things: What Categories Reveal About the Mind* (Chicago: University of Chicago Press, 1987).

only have to watch some of the good popular music videos of Paul Simon and Peter Gabriel (e.g., "René Magritte and his Dog After the War" and "Sledgehammer") to recognize that for this emergent culture, reality is not something you adapt to or reflect in *mimesis;* it is something you constellate by getting it all together: no matter whether the "it" is pixels or people.

The inclusion of Buddhist philosophy and practice into Varela's approach to cognitive science seems to have come about as a result of his having to flee Pinochet's Chile to return to the United States in 1974 to take up a position as Assistant Professor at the University of Colorado's Medical School in Denver.[30] Once again Varela found himself in the center of a cultural transformation, for by 1974 the counterculture was beginning to move beyond the escape into hippie communes to the formation of new alternative institutions. In 1974 the Tibetan Buddhist teacher Chögyam Trungpa Rinpoche established his Naropa Institute in nearby Boulder, Colorado, where Varela was living. To catch the attention of Americans, this most unorthodox refugee from Tibet chose a path not of piety but "crazy wisdom" in which he appeared to be something of a cross between a Central Asian shaman and a drunken Dylan Thomas. This style of presentation seemed to be peculiarly effective and charismatic, especially for people fleeing the piety of orthodox religion or the bureaucratic rationality of science, for the Rinpoche was able to inspire gifted minds as different as the New York poet Allen Ginsberg, the English physicist Jeremy Hayward, and the Chilean neurophysiologist Francisco Varela. Perhaps because they were both political refugees, Trungpa and Varela felt an affinity for one another that deepened over the years until by the time of Trungpa's death in 1987, Varela himself had developed from being a student to becoming a lecturer at the various Dharma Dhatu centers in North America and Europe.

---

[30] See Francisco Varela, "Reflections on the Chilean Civil War" in *Lindisfarne Letter* 8, Winter 1979, pp. 13–19.

For a cognitive scientist the meticulous analysis of states of mind in Abidharma psychology must have been an amazing revelation, especially to someone who had been taught to believe with Heidegger that philosophy was the exclusive creation of the Greeks. But in the study of Indian and Tibetan schools of thought, Varela could see that there were other ways to approach a critique of "the metaphysics of presence." For a scientist at work in challenging the whole notion of "representation," this exposure to traditional Asian cultures as well as to the North American counterculture came in perfect timing for the autopoiesis of his own imagination. With G. Spenser Brown lecturing on "the Laws of Form" at Esalen in California, and Gregory Bateson lecturing on "Mind in Nature" at Lindisfarne in New York, Varela began to move back and forth between the academic Establishment and the para-academic counterculture. Out of this milieu of the 1970s came his book, *Principles of Biological Autonomy*.

Varela's response to his historical environment was certainly autopoietic and not at all predictable. In the humanities it is often easy to see how scholarship is a form of disguised autobiography, but perhaps this is equally true for science and only the camouflage of mathematics makes it difficult to see the life history of the scientist encoded within the hieratic script. In normal science an organism resides in the container of the environment to which it must adapt, and this certainly describes the life of a professor in the containing institution of a university; but in Varela's biology, and in Varela's personal life history, the organism is an evolutionary process of "natural drift." If the nervous system is operationally closed, it means that the organism encounters its uniquely specified environment on its own terms, and that, in fact, the organism is not an object in an environmental container but an evolutionary process in a natural historical space that is almost what one could call a cultural extension of itself. Just as a Frenchman lives in a linguistic domain that shapes his behavior, so does a bird, a bee, or a dolphin live in a cognitive domain that is its existential field, its world. This world is not a container, an external environment in which it is simply located; rather, it is more like the magnetic fields or Van Allen Belts that emanate from our planet.

To visualize this change of narrative, one has to change one's imaginative landscape. Instead of seeing the object in Newtonian space, the beaver in a pond, one should envision the organism with an imagery of fluid dynamics, with patterns of turbulent flow through time in which the natural history of the organism is at play with the open and undetermined path of its evolutionary present and future. This stream of turbulence is a relationship between constraint and creativity precisely in the way in which the art of ballet is a relationship between gravity and grace. The environment does not contain the organism and constrain it to adapt or die; the environment is the sum of all the collective flows of the organisms that constitute it. One organism evolves by climbing on the back of another; together the pathways of their natural histories in time constitute an evolutionary landscape.

Scientists who think in the visual terms of the nonlinear dynamics of complex systems do not seem to have as much difficulty in effecting this shift of the imagination, and biologists, such as the embryologist Stuart Kaufman at the University of Pennsylvania, are currently exploring just such problems at the Santa Fe Institute for the Study of Complex Systems. Kaufman, unlike Gunther Stent, does seem to be able to imagine a new world view. He takes Varela's work quite seriously, for he sees the dynamics of self-organizing systems to be constitutive of "the adaptive landscapes" in which organisms evolve on the backs of one another.[31] Population geneticists have a much harder time effecting this post-Darwinian shift, for they require a flater space in which the distribution of genotype and phenotype can be calculated in linear equations. Unfortunately when these biologists have to study whole

---

[31] See Stuart Kaufman in *Understanding Origin: Scientific Ideas on the Origin of Life, Mind, and Society*, Ed., Francisco Varela (Stanford, Calif.: Stanford University Press, forthcoming).

ecosystems to calculate the population balance between prey and predator, they re-express the old three-body problem from physics and become mired down in such overwhelming complexity that they can only respond in frustration and exasperation by flattening everything in immense oversimplifications and linear simulations. The shift from linear to nonlinear dynamics is more than a change of attitude, it is a radical shift from an algebraic to a geometrical imagination.[32]

3. FROM POSTMODERNISM TO PLANETARY CULTURE

THE BIOLOGY OF Varela is truly radical in every sense of the word, for the scientific world it calls forth is quite different from the world of power through manipulation at MIT and Harvard. The "enactive" cognitive science of Varela expresses an immanental world of "codependent origination." The cognitivist view of the mind in Fodor and Pylyshyn is a split Cartesian world of mental symbols and meat. Because the computational symbols are transcendent to meat, the mathematical knowledge of them generates a scientific elite that is equally transcendent to the meatheads of the general polity. There is no choice in this, and, not surprisingly, the engineers and their journalistic apologists always present their inventions as an inevitable destiny. As Stewart Brand says in praise of MIT: "Once a new technology rolls over you, if you're not part of the steamroller, you're part of the road."[33]

---

[32] See James Gleick, *Chaos: Making a New Science* (New York: Viking, 1987). The subtext to this very interesting work is the return of a geometrical imagination to contemporary science, and the role of the outsider, individuals such as Feigenbaum and Mandelbrot, in effecting this shift away from the linear and algebraic mentalities of the ruling scientific bureaucracies.

[33] See Stewart Brand, *The Media Lab: Inventing the Future at MIT* (New York: Viking, 1987), p. 9.

The culture of hackers, engineers, and cognitive scientists at MIT brings forth a very peculiar and most unsensuous world of abstraction, laboratory ugliness, and an electronic *umwelt* of noise, fluorescent lights and cathode tubes radiating organisms without stop. The computer terminals are never turned off, for electronic noise is the environment of choice for engineers; like an unconscious psychic musak, it serves as a universal solvent that breaks down the resistance of the flesh. It is an unhealthy place for an old-fashioned evolutionary human body to be, and it reminds me of the "progressive" shoe stores of the fifties in which we as children could twinkle our toes in the X-ray machines. In the future, we will probably see a whole syndrome of related diseases, mental and physical, that will come out of places like the Media Lab at MIT, where this invisible environment of electronic noise is so overpowering.[34]

It is, however, only invisible to someone who is insensitive, unsensuous, and possessed by abstractions: namely, your average North American computer hacker and engineer. But these are precisely the people who are claiming to be "inventing the future at MIT" and who wish to extend their environment so that in the future our cities will not be Tuscan hill towns with piazzas and cafes, sunshine and bright wine, culturally celebrative people in equally delightful buildings from which come forth hand-wrought food and real espresso, but rather military-industrial space stations serving instant coffee in carcinogenic Styrofoam cups and where as much attention will be grudgingly paid to the body as is now in a restroom or restaurant in an American airport.

There is a culture, a sociology, and a politics to knowledge, and Maturana and Varela's language gives them away as ones who are not likely to be of use in upholding the structures of the dominant scientific and technical elite. To speak of "auto-

---

[34] Ibid., p. 35.

poiesis," of "the bringing forth of worlds," or of systems of self-organization in which there is "a coming together in mutual satisfaction without anybody being in control"[35] does not call to mind either life in Cambridge or the scientific politics of the industrial nation-state.

> If we know that our world is necessarily the world we bring forth with others, every time we are in conflict with another human being with whom we want to remain in coexistence, we cannot affirm what for us is certain (an absolute truth) because that would negate the other person. If we want to coexist with the other person, we must see that his certainty—however undesirable it may seem to us—is as legitimate and valid as our own because, like our own, that certainty expresses his conservation of structural coupling in a domain of existence—however undescribable it may seem to us. Hence, the only possibility for coexistence is to opt for a broader perspective in which both parties fit in the bringing forth of a common world.[36]

The loss of the idea of representation, along with its descendent of the idea of adaptation, can be linked to the loss of the political power of scientific elites, for elites are supposed to be adequate representations of an objective world, and this world is not supposed to be open to change or multiple unfoldments.[37]. It is a fixed and absolute world of "natural law" and the scientist is precisely the one who "has unlocked nature's secrets" and has the keys to the powers of control. The scientist is the one who represents natural law within society, and, therefore, it makes absolutely perfect sense to him that the scientist should have power to bring society into har-

[35] Francisco Varela, "Color Vision and Cognition," address to the Lindisfarne Fellows, Tarrytown Conference Center, May 3, 1986.

[36] Maturana and Varela, *The Tree of Knowledge,* pp. 245, 246.

[37] See Francisco Varela, "Laying Down a Path in Walking" in *Gaia, The Political Implications of the New Biology,* Ed., W. I. Thompson (Great Barrington, Mass.: Lindisfarne Press, 1987), pp. 48–64.

mony with this natural law that only he understands. This development, of course, means to bring the wild under control, and to bring the nonscientific areas of humanity under scientific management. Skinnerian behaviorism was always quite open about this societal ambition, and so now is sociobiology. If genetic engineering and artificial intelligence can succeed in their various projects to take over evolution and replace natural selection with cultural selection, and replace ecologies of mind with the controlled intelligence of machines, then Cambridge, U.S.A., will literally become the Vatican of a One, holy, catholic, and academic church.

What is undermining the absolutist ground under this kind of authoritarian science is the imagination of a new kind of science that is expressed in the cognitive biology of Maturana and Varela, the nonlinear dynamics of Gaia in the geophysiology of Lovelock and Margulis, the chemistry of Prigogine,[38] and the chaos dynamics of the new topologists. If the universe is open and undetermined, and if multiple worlds are possible within a turbulent flow of natural drift, then life is precisely a dialogue between chaos and order. Like a surfer riding a wave of turbulence, life may ride the waves of chemistry and physics, but its behavior is not at all predictable from chemistry or physics. This openness works to enhance novelty and innovation and unpredictability to make a universe much more than a deterministic machine.[39] Thus, paradoxically, Varela's thesis that "Every autonomous system is operationally closed"[40] results, rather whimsically, in a universe of openness. Small disturbances can accumulate, and the

---

[38] See Ilya Prigogine and Isabelle Stenger's *Order out of Chaos: Man's New Dialogue With Nature* (New York: Bantam, 1984).

[39] "Chaos imposes fundamental limits on prediction." See "Chaos" by James P. Crutchfield, J. Doyne Framer, Norman H. Packard, and Robert Shaw in *Scientific American,* Dec. 1986, pp. 46–57.

[40] Francisco Varela, *Principles of Biological Autonomy* (New York: Elsevier Holland, 1979), p. 58.

cumulative effect is to unfold a world. But there is not one world, but infinitely possible and mutually interpenetrating worlds. With the enactive cognitive science of Varela, we have moved out of the tight elitist containers of an objective world into the fascinating realms of Mind of Borges, Lem, and Calvino in contemporary literature, or into the ancient and visionary cosmologies of the Hwa Yen Sutra of Indian and Chinese Buddhism in which "innumerable universes tremble at the tip of Buddha's hair." If there is ambiguity, relativity, and fractal complexity all the way down to the fine strands of Buddha's hair, there is also wonder, mystery, confusion, and creativity: in other words there is the cognitive domain of Life in which science as knowing (*sciens*) leads not to power and uncompassionate manipulations but to insight, understanding, and compassion for all sentient beings that can suffer.

Were the linear reductionists in the tradition of Skinner to Wilson to Minsky to succeed in making Cambridge the Vatican of a new planetary scientific medievalism, then noise, complexity, and novelty would be eliminated as a wholly predictable and controlled world would be brought forth in their linguistic domain. Inevitably, this kind of science would overproduce the trivia of its own ecclesiastical bureaucracy, and what Stuart Kaufman calls "a complexity catastrope" would be generated from the cumulative effects of repressed noise and small disturbances within the planetary church of the One True Science. Depending on the political empowerments of this science, this situation could result in a breakdown that could be a new Renaissance or a new Dark Ages. We should give thanks, therefore, that we now live in a historical situation in which science does not have this kind of cultural power.

An art gallery in which all the paintings were mirrors would be boring, and so would a world with only one reflection of existence. There is not simply one objective world, one fixed ground with adequate representations of it in mind; there are multiple worlds in an ecology of multiple biomes and organisms, each constituting cognitive domains of fascinating richness. Those who can live with ambiguity, complexity, and infinite variety can rejoice that there are windows to different worlds in the cognition of an antibody, a bee, a dolphin, a bird, a human, an elemental, or an angel. The reductionists of scientific orthodoxy are like those Reformation fanatics who wished to close down the theaters and pull out the statues from the churches; for those hysterical puritans the sensory complexity of the world was intolerable and they wished to flatten it into the black and white deadness of their own imaginations. Ironically, these religious fanatics were the true followers of Newton and wished to live in a world in which there was only the idea of God set against the black and white void of objects stripped of their sensory qualities and ruled by a universal law of gravity as they circled about the deity in a dark Newtonian space.

Anglo-American science has triumphed through a particular feigning maneuvre of specialization that pretends to be stripped of subjectivity, value systems, and philosophy, but consistently advances a methodology of reductionism that amounts to a program of cultural elimination. By contrast, the continental European approach is often one of generalists, or the person gifted in more than his narrow speciality; so an Einstein will also be a violinist, a Heisenberg will be a pianist, a Wittgenstein will be a gifted architect. French philosophers, such as Merleau-Ponty or Michel Serres, write with a literary sense of style and have interesting things to say about art as well as science. The philosopher in this tradition is not a technician, but a person of deep culture, and it is just this sense of a linguistic and sensuous tradition, be it French, German, or Italian, that is missing in the technical orientation so favored by the American engineering approach to cognition. It is almost a form of class warfare in which a lower-middle class is suspicious of the culture of the upper-middle class that makes it feel so inferior and uncomfortable, so European philosophy is dismissed as obfuscation, self-indulgence, and unscientific mystification. The kind of American Big Science that makes it in the big laboratories of the big state universities has no time to mess around with all this phoney stuff, so it thrives as a boys club of computer hackers staying up all night in the lab and stuffing themselves with junk food and Coca-Cola.

The positive side to this American culture is a "no bull shit" commitment to experience. Europeans can be content to substitute discourse for experience to discuss yoga over cognac and cigars in the men's-club setting that has become the television set for Vienna's popular talk show, *Club Zwei*. For the German and French traditions, discourse *is* experience and a performance of the culture, and no gentleman need take philosophy any further than words to twist himself into a pretzel in the practice of yoga, or to stay up all night inventing some maniacally whimsical virus for software programs. The Germans will be heavy and leaden, but serious; and the French will be elegant figure skaters entranced with the surface of things, but whatever the European style, experience will be considered simply as a springboard for discourse. Parisian radio gives itself away just as much as Viennese television, for a three-minute song will be played for only a minute and a half so that the announcers can discuss it for ten. And what is true of popular culture is true for high culture, for Derrida and Habermass, though opposed to one another, still express the same "deep structure" in which life is simply a pretext for a text. Given these cultural differences, it is not surprising that Maturana and Varela's book *The Tree of Knowledge* is a bestseller in Germany, but not in the United States, and that North Americans tend to be suspicious that their South American biology is just so much disguised European palaver that cannot cut it in the real world of hard science. The fact that Varela has chosen to work in Paris, rather than in the United States, indicates a lingering association to the phenomenological traditions that he encountered as a teenager, but his continuing work with colleagues in the United States also indicates a desire to straddle the Atlantic and not to accept the centuries-old dichotomy between Anglo-American

Empiricism and Continental Rationalism but to find a way to use America to protect himself from Europe, and Europe to protect himself from America.

When one steps back to take in the relationship of Varela's thinking on the operational closure of the cell in autopoiesis, in neuronal assemblies in organisms, and in the immune system as a cognitive domain, there is a both such a large scale of thought and such a detailed focus on the particulars of research that his work has a very impressive architechtonic indeed. We are no longer dealing with piecemeal contributions to research, but a revisioning of biology in which perception theory in neurophysiology, the cellular dynamics of life, and the phenomenology of the immune system are all coordinated into a profoundly different philosophy of Life, one that in its global combination of scientific method and Buddhist practice amounts to a new historical mentality as large as that in the shift from medievalism to modernism.

We could call this new mentality postmodernism, but as this term is used to describe the return of historical quotation and beaux art decoration to architecture, and absolutely anything in philosophy after Paris, 1968, I prefer to avoid that well-worn but undescriptive term. For lack of a better term, I have preferred, since 1971, to identify this transition as the shift from postindustrial society to planetary culture.[41]

If we North Americans rest easy in our conviction that "the future is being invented at MIT," planetary culture will not be an ecology of multiple cognitive domains; it will be an abstract system of intellectual dominion, a space station with cyborgs attending to the void. The journey of Francisco Varela has not been to outer space, but his intellectual odyssey from Heidegger in his teens to Maturana in his twenties and Chögyam Trungpa Rinpoche in his thirties shows a blending

---

[41] See W. I. Thompson, *At the Edge of History* (New York: Harper & Row, 1971), pp. 26 and 142; and *Passages About Earth: An Exploration of the New Planetary Culture* (New York: Harper & Row, 1974).

of North and South, East and West, that amounts to one of the more planetary landscapes of our time. Together with Lovelock and Margulis, he has so affected the contemporary counterculture that a planetary culture or a "new age" without a new science is inconceivable. Unlike many of the New-Agers who have chosen to become ex-scientists to enjoy the admiration of people who were never scientists to begin with, Lovelock, Margulis, and Varela have chosen the harder work of remaining in the laboratory in dialogue with their skeptical colleagues, and that is "the difference that makes a difference" between science and self-indulgence. Science is a world unto itself and to touch the heart of science one must work from within, so those who have in compassion chosen to remain within may in fact be giving us our last chance to bring forth a biology worthy of life.

CHAPTER FOUR

A CULTURAL
HISTORY OF
CONSCIOUSNESS

HISTORY IS AN IMAGINARY LANDSCAPE—A TABLEAU of battles for some, a mural of scientific discoveries and technological inventions for others; and for those who avert their eyes from horizons of mystery or hallways of propaganda, there still remains an internal cinema of unconsciously edited perceptions in which self is the *figure* and nature the *ground*. Consciousness itself, as either a Buddhist heap (*skandha*) or a scientific narrative, is a landscape, for one cannot know without a world. More basic even than the Kantian categories of space and time is the world, for as Heidegger has argued, the relationship between existence and world is not that of contained and container, but the world as it is "cast forth" in the very process of existing itself.[1]

---

[1] "To exist means, among other things, to cast forth a world, and in fact in such a way that with the throwness of this projection, with the factial existence of a Dasein, extant entities are always already uncovered." Martin Heidegger, *The Basic Problems of Phenomenology,* Trans. Albert Hofstadter (Bloomington, Ill.: Indiana University Press, 1982), p. 168.

In this capacity of bringing forth a world, we are utterly incapable of doing it alone, for it requires others to enable us to be ourselves. Language ability may be innate, but if humans are raised in the wild, as was the case of the famous "wolf children," they cannot ever bring forth language if it is not developed in infancy.[2] We cannot become human without the society of humans, for we are not human in and of ourselves, and there really is no such thing as a Cartesian ego contemplating the universe in solitude. Sartre was wrong when he said: "Hell is others"; rather, hell is precisely the lack of others, the pure void without a world. Nothing of us is really alone, for we share our body with bacteria and viruses, and we share our mind with neurons that Lynn Margulis thinks might be evolutionarily captured spirochetes, and as well with other minds in the ecology of languages and cultures that constitute our world.

The solitary and competent ego is a fiction, but even a "fact" is a fiction, for a fact without a world is like a flame without an atmosphere. When we have truly grasped the illusionary nature of the Self, walled around with its private property, then our notion of a polity will change as we culturally evolve from an aggregation of individuals suspicious of others to the planetary community of Life. In many ways, we Americans deceive ourselves when we see ours as the most advanced nation on earth, for the United States, with its distrust of community, its rejection of taxes for schools and streetcars and trains, is still an immature culture. Ours is a society still all too close to its pioneer stage of leveling the forests, mining resources, and trying to stand off the intrusions of government to amass private wealth at the expense of the ecological and social fabric of the biosphere.

If the solitary ego separate from the immanental context

---

[2] See Humberto Maturana and Francisco Varela, *The Tree of Knowledge: The Biological Roots of Human Understanding* (Boston: New Science Library, 1986), pp. 128–131.

that brings it forth, is an illusion, equally illusionary is the idea that there is a cognitive system of abstract symbols that is separate from the flesh of the sentient beings that interact in their cognitive domains. Some philosophers from Pythagoras to Descartes to Kant, and now on to Fodor and Pylyshyn, fancy that there is a secret transcendent code, be it eidos, number, or pure computation lurking in the darkness. Like a searchlight that has heard rumors about a mysterious darkness and probes the sky in search of it, these men keep hoping to find the final code that will crack the secrets of the universe. There are others, fewer and far less influential thinkers in our society, who sense that that search is endless precisely because it treats experience as illusion and seeks to escape experience with some illusionary experience. For those who think otherwise, neither idealism nor realism makes sense of the way in which we make sense *with* the world. As webs come out of spiders, or breath forms in frozen air, worlds come out of us. As in the condition of world making in which Wordsworth's nurse sings a song as she cradles him by the banks of the Derwent, we are from birth brought forth into a world of mind. And if we appreciated the importance of this primary act of bringing forth a world in the condition of birth, then our society would change as the foundational institution of childbirth changed.[3]

What frames and defines a world is the act of participating in a context. To take part in something is to take a part from

---

[3] To appreciate the horror of a "normal" birth in an American hospital maternity ward, one should see Bill Viola's video "Silent Life" from *The Reflecting Pool* (1979). If one knows better, and has experienced natural childbirth after the philosophy of Dr. Frederick Leboyer, this is an extremely painful video to watch. In this fifteen-minute study, we listen to the voiceovers of two nurses gossiping as the infants, who are ignored, untouched, and completely alienated from their mothers, struggle to make sense of their incarceration. It is not all that great a distance to move from the insensitivity of the nurses to the humanity of the infants to the insensitivity of military police to the humanity of their political prisoners. As opposed to Sartre's vision of hell as others, this is a vision of hell in which the others are gone and one is left in complete aloneness.

an immensity of possibilities. One fixes one's attention and that opens up possibilities: just as when we open a file with a personal computer and watch the screen fill out with the desired world, there are innumerable other files, but each must fill the screen of the limits of our attention and exclude the others that are, for all our ignoring them, still "there." If one releases one's way of fixing attention on the conventional world, other modes of taking part begin to become possible. Meditation or death have ways of unfixing the world, madness as well, but the very multiplicity of innumerable universes can send us back in fear to what we know and hold to be true.

We think that we need a landscape as a ground to sustain us. If we study the patterns moving on the surface of a river, we need a bank or a bridge to keep us suspended in meditation. And even at the shore of our tidal breath in less topological forms of meditation, we find ourselves coming back to a certain body of knowledge that is the landscape of our world, a world with, perhaps, a few new territories added to its map.

Gaia is a new landscape, a new way of knowing the planet and worlding our way with it. It is as large and imaginatively provocative for our era as Darwinian evolution was for our great-grandparent's time. And by "Gaia" I do not mean only Jim Lovelock's interpretation of his own discoveries. I mean, rather, a dynamic geometry of planetary behavior that is synchronically experienced, as if one were listening to a Beethoven string quartet, by hearing the instruments of Abraham, Lovelock, Margulis, and Varela all at the same time in a new mental space that is larger than their books taken singly. First, one sees the films of the microcosm of Margulis, sees the tubulins, spirochetes, and neurons in the motile dance of life, and understands what Buddha saw when he found "Self" empty but individuality richly full of universal relatedness in countless dimensions. Second, one hears Lovelock's gentle voice speaking of the fluid dynamics of the ocean, the atmosphere, and the slowly moving tectonic plates, and accepts how the planetary bioplasm of bacteria could give rise to this larger dance through its polluting life and the generosity of its fecundating death. Third, one envisions these dancing patterns of oscillating spirochetes, gaseous clouds, and floating tectonic plates in the dynamic imagery of Abraham, and senses that it probably does not stop with Earth, but goes on to include the solar wind and the geometry of the behavior of the entire solar system, and on to unimaginable galactic complexities. And as the mind boggles, one hears the entry of the instrumental voice of Varela speaking of the mind itself, from the lowest prebiotic molecules to the highest mathematics as "the organization of the living," and one begins to appreciate how Varela gives us the "metadynamic" to understand the nature of "emergence," that an emergent system is more than a net of linear feedback loops. As we move in and out of all these cognitive domains, the instrumental lines become harmonic and the whole takes part in it all. That is what I mean by "Gaia."

As we ponder the dynamics of cognition in the immune system of an animal or of a planet, we have to learn to imagine what we cannot see at these microcosmic and macrocosmic levels of time and space. And so the value of the imagination returns to challenge the reductionist mentality of modernism that ruled during the period of the mechanization of the world picture. A new mentality has historically arrived and its new view of the world is so profoundly different that it makes us suspect that the very process by which historical mentalities are brought forth is part of a cultural evolution of consciousness in which the adaptive landscape we extrude has moved us out of one world and into a different universe. The world this new biology brings forth repositions humanity: neither the scum of an accident on a freakish planet nor the pinnacle of cosmic evolution, humanity is only one form of Mind of which there are innumerable varieties in the immanence of order and the emergence of novelty.

This new biology that I have sketched in an imaginary landscape drew me into it, precisely because it was not only a theory, but a new world view. If we appreciate Lovelock's understanding of the atmosphere, then we can begin to sense that there are most likely new discoveries awaiting us in the next century: new perceptions of how the cycles of the sun may affect the periodicities of the earth in its reversals of magnetic field or its cycle of ice ages. And if there is a dynamic to our planet and the sun, we can begin to suspect that the entire topological arrangement of the solar system in its movement through galactic space has something to teach us about cosmic cycles that we have only glimpsed in myth and science fiction. And as our imaginations move from the vastness of the macrocosm to the subvisible bacteria studied by Margulis, our new understanding of the symbiotic architecture of the cell means that the architecture of our future cities will change as pollution itself is made into the living membrane that joins human and microbial communities in forms of cooperation in which the "factories" become more like the wilderness and the wild becomes bacterially cultured. As we move back and forth between these domains of the large and the small, our appreciation of Mind as "the organization of the living" will also suggest to us that the computers of the future need not be industrial nightmares of Robocops, but the opposite, silicon and viral trellises on which the universal Mind can flower. To see the universe as more than a container, to see cities in which human and microbial life are not suburbs and slums, to see a new animism in which topological angels interact with the elementals of our carbon- and silicon-based computers, we need imagination. And before we can ever hope to be open to the scientific imagination of the future, we have to be open to the imagination of the mythologies and arts of the past. If we look on myth as gibberish and art as illusion, our science will be brutal and will brutalize others in the inappropriate organization of our social institutions. The Buddhist understanding of compassion that is expressed in Varela's cognitive biology is not accidental but essential to the nature of understanding. We have been so habituated to the kind of science brought forth by the Dr. Tellers of our military-industrial world, men who now insist that we explode nuclear weapons in orbit to generate the X-ray lasers that can kill rockets and satellites, men who seek to reorganize the entire world economy to sustain their destruction of the connective tissue of space and Earth, that we have lost our capacity to imagine another way for science to be. It will take a new mentality to know the Earth and bring forth a new world with a new planetary culture.

As we experience the novelty of this new mentality, we need to look back and construct a history, not of battles or technological inventions, but of the emergence of mentalities. This glance backward at history takes in a "longue durée" that dwarfs the millennia of the Mediterranean studied by Brendel[4]; it is not the *mentalité collective* of the *Annalistes* concerned with the ordinary man rather than the military hero or the artistic and scientific genius; it is a more Gaian perspective of a cultural ecology in which humanity is only one inhabitant; it is a cultural evolutionary perspective in which the primary mentality of the human "structural coupling" of mind and nature is transformed. This concept of mentality is more fundamental and is much closer to the idea of mentality in the work of an earlier French thinker, Lucien Lévy-Bruhl and his concept of *"la mentalité primitive."*[5]

---

[4] See Fernand Braudel, *Écrits sur l'histoire* (Paris: Flammarion, 1969), p. 41.

[5] See Lucien Lévy-Bruhl, *Primitive Mentality*, trans. Lillian A. Clare (1923, reprint ed.; New York: AMS Press, Inc., 1976). When I was an undergraduate, the name of Lévy-Bruhl was always pronounced in lectures with a snarl of contempt, for Lévy-Bruhl was seen to be part of a Eurocentric, imperialistic anthropology that considered primitives to be relics of an earlier, prescientific level of development. I was told that it was wrong to make generalizations about "primitives and children," but when I read Wordsworth and Piaget, Lévy-Bruhl and Redfield, it was the cultural construction of reality and the transformation of world views through societal changes that fascinated me and seemed to suggest that if primitives and children did not think alike, they each had a mentality that was quite other to the accepted one. I could not articulate then, as I have tried to do in this book, just why this mentality of modernism did not seem to map the world I lived in. Like Varela, I too wanted to study "the role of Mind in the Universe," but I was not so fortunate in finding a teacher like Maturana. I knew that I did not agree with my teachers, so I set about trying to find just what a mentality was by looking at its edges, hoping there to find how one world view changes into another. I studied the shift from hunting and gathering to agriculture, and from

On the eastern horizon, the mental space of the "dawn" of humanity, we have the emergence of human culture in the Pleistocene; on the western horizon of the obscure future, we have what Chardin called "the planetization of mankind." From 200,000 B.C. with the first appearance of decorated tools to 2000 A.D., we have a bounded mental space that we construe to be the place of our historical dwelling. Between these two horizons, the events we choose to single out tell us more about us than about our ancestors. Technologists focus on technologies, artists focus on art, soldiers focus on battles, politicians focus on changing political structures from hunting band to nation-state, and priests focus on the lives of prophets and messiahs. The defining event may be the invention of fire or the Incarnation, but either way the idea is that there is an event that changes everything.

The concept of "emergence" takes the opposite perspective. There is no climactic event on a single day in which a cyanobacterium says to itself, "I shall fart oxygen and make me an atmosphere." In the scramble of life in natural drift,

---

agricultural to industrial, never believing the Marxist cultural historians like V. Gordon Childe that it could all be explained in terms of technological revolutions. My professors of philosophy frowned on my interest in Whitehead; my professors of literature frowned on my desire to discuss Wordsworth and Piaget and gestalt psychology in an English class; and my professors of anthropology frowned on my interest in Cassirer and Lévy-Bruhl. Not one of them had the common sense to tell me to go and read Vico, and so I was forced to reinvent the Viconian wheel as I came up with a grand theory of cultural change that suggested that there were four stages to the progression of a culture. I had not heard of Vico's Gods, Heroes, Men, Chaos, so I used the terms taken from Heinz Werner's gestalt psychology and called them Diffuse, Articulate, Discrete, and Syncretic. I should have called them, more artistically, Archaic, Classic, Baroque, and Archaistic. In a mere two hundred pages of an undergraduate Honors Thesis that my professors derided as my Summa Anthropological-Philosophica, but still allowed me to write, I tried to show that the evolution of styles in ancient Greek statuary, Middle American Mayan architecture, and English poetry, all revealed the same structural pattern. The thrill of discovering a theory and the fun of articulating it in a book-length thesis was a joy of coming of age, a feeling of becoming a man and doing my own work, instead of being like all the other students, writing a thesis on the work of a single philosopher or poet.

One can get away with this sort of thing in a good liberal arts college, but there is no chance of it in the professional-training or graduate school. By then, thanks to Joyce's *Finnegan's Wake,* I had heard of Vico and found out that I wasn't ahead of my

photosynthesis is one response to the presence of light, and since it produces energy and releases oxygen as a by-product, it goes on its way. Obviously, no one noticed or could know that such activity was constituent of a new Epoch. Probably the activity at the time might seem as irrelevant to the atmospheric status quo as the first automobiles were to horses. "Emergence" is, by its very nature, the description of an observer who is outside the cognitive domain of the behavior he or she is describing in the terms of their knowing. The description constitutes a recursive support of the observer's own world picture.

So here I sit, looking at the screen of a Macintosh and in imagination, rolling the screen of history back and forth. Instructed by the natural history of life, I suspect that what I am looking for are not "events," but thresholds of emergence that are also projections of my own framing of perceptions. I see an emergent mentality dividing me from my MIT colleagues and associating me with my Lindisfarne friends, and I imagine in time a similar emergence separating the artists and scientists of the Renaissance from the leaders of the Church. I no-

---

time, but, in fact, quite a bit behind it. Lévy-Strauss and structuralism was the fashion in graduate school then, for deconstructionism had not yet been imported. But whether one was a New Critic, a bibliographer, or a structuralist, there was a shared agreement in 1964 that the historical study of a text was definitely the wrong approach; thinking otherwise, I went off to Dublin to study the Insurrection of 1916 as a way of understanding the role of imagination in the construction of historical reality. I thought that perhaps my undergraduate professors might be pleased if they knew that instead of studying the meaning of all cultures everywhere, I was finally specializing by studying one week in one city.

Now twenty-five years after trying to construct a "Philosophy of World View," I find myself coming around again to considering the nature of the human mentality and its changes through time. *Now, of course, I would no longer believe in one single theory that could transform the complexity of a planetary ecology into a single linear progression.* Now a theory would be more of interest as one narrative among many, one novel among a library of others, for it is the act of constructing an imaginary landscape of history that is exciting, just as once before it was the intellectual thrill of constructing a theory that was exciting. If the theory was wrong, well then, what does that mean? All theories of history, Marxian, Freudian, Foucaultian, or whatever, are "wrong"; but as exercises in intellectual mythology they become cultural performances. Small wonder that political cultures and academic subcultures have grown up around them and have taken their stories to become history.

tice that this shift from medievalism to modernism was not simply about a movement from religion to art to science, but a large transformation that included a shift from script to print, from the world church to the world economy, from kingdom to industrial nation-state. The events that are highlighted in traditional historical narratives seem to be morphemes in a grammar of a language that holds them together in significant ways, so that new technologies, new ideologies, and new polities come forth together.

If we make the emergence of these clusters, rather than single events, the focus of our attention, what other clusters have there been in this mental space between 200,000 B.C. and 2000 A.D.?

First there was the emergence of human culture, then the emergence of human society with agriculture, then the emergence of civilization in the Middle East, India, and China and the Americas, then the emergence of industrialization in 1500 with its new global economy,[6] and now the emergence of planetization. So, there we have it, a narrative of five emergences, each with five mentalities externalizing themselves in five polities.

   I.   Culture (Paleolithic to Neolithic, 200,000 to 10,000 B.C.)
   II. Society (10,000 to 3500 B.C.)
   III. Civilization (3500 B.C. to 1500 A.D.)
   IV. Industrialization (1500 to 1945)
   V.   Planetization (1945 to ———?)

---

[6] The eighteenth-century Industrial Revolution in Great Britain has been over-emphasized. As Fernand Braudel has noted: "With the coming of steam, the pace of the West increased as if by magic. But the magic can be explained: it had been prepared and made possible in advance. To paraphrase a historian (Pierre Léon), first came evolution (a slow rise) and then revolution (an acceleration); two connected movements." in *Civilization and Capitalism, Vol. I. The Structures of Everyday Life* (London: Collins, 1981), p. 372.

In Culture, the form of polity is the hunting and gathering band. In Society, gathering extends itself into gardening first and later into agriculture, but in its formative stages this differentiated society is still matrilineal. When literate civilization is brought forth, then the polity is first the city-state, then the city-state extended into an empire. With the rise of capitalism in the Renaissance, the extension of the city-state becomes a financial empire more than a military one, and a new marriage of technology to capitalism begins to challenge the traditional wedding of military technology to agriculture as the landed knights no longer begin to wield as much power as the bankers and merchants in Florence, Venice, or Antwerp. This formation climaxes in the growth of the new middle-class polity of the industrial nation-state. Ultimately, the defense of the nation-state stimulates an acceleration of technology into aerospace and this brings enemies closer together in the forms of transnational planetization we now see expressed in the relations between the U.S.A. and the U.S.S.R.

In the movement from Band to Society to Civilization to Industrialization and finally to Planetization, there is a dialectical progression in which previous entities are not eliminated but reconstituted in a new integration. It is a process very much like the evolution of the cell as described by Lynn Margulis in which the motility of the spirochete is captured to serve as the transport system for chromosones, or in which the organelles, such as the mitochondria and chloroplasts, are captured to serve as energy producers within the new giant of the conglomerate cell. The hunting band does not disappear in matrilineal Society, it becomes the male bonding of the ritual animal quest or the raiding party. When the walled compound grows into the city-state and when defense requires standing armies, rather than mothers' brothers dropping their hoes and picking up their swords and bows to protect the tribe, then agricultural technology becomes highly specialized and increasingly male. The male with his animals and plow is invited into the garden to plow the labial furrows with his phallic tool, and the elaborate system of irrigation that floods the field is mythologized as male. In the Sumerian language, "water" and "semen" are the same word, and are united in the personage of the male water god, Enki. When this new male technology of irrigation and walled defense entirely surrounds Society, then matrilineal society becomes domesticated to become the conservative hearth gods of the household and the mystery school of the matron and the maiden that survives alongside the changing empires of warriors.

In Industrialization, when Capitalism brings in a new world order, civilization does not disappear, it becomes the mystery school of the elite, the still-feudal establishment of knighthood that must decorate the vulgar business of the newly rich. Industrial England with its capitalistic empire as the structure, but its feudal system as the content expresses this dialectic perfectly.

Now that we are moving from a civilian economy supported by the sale of automobiles and television sets to a scientific economy, the nation-state is becoming the new organelle within the cell. Like a chloroplast, Japan, for example, produces an enormous amount of energy in the form of capital, but this venture capital is used for the scientific investment in the nationally coordinated Fifth-Generation Computer Project, and the product of this enterprise is so costly that no civilian could ever hope to be the customer. This product is not a Toyota or a Sony VCR for the home but a computer that enables nation-states to design better jet fighters, or nation-states to buy up other nation-states in transnational mergers, such as the U.S.S.R., to take on the exploration of the planets.[7]

The nation-state is now what the corporation was in the nineteenth and early twentieth century. One now holds currencies and speculates with them in the same manner one did with stocks before. Like commodity-futures, nation-state "fu-

---

[7] See W. I. Thompson, "Gaia and the Politics of Life: A Program for the Nineties?" in *Gaia: A Way of Knowing* (Great Barrington, Mass.: Lindisfarne Press, 1987), pp. 167–214.

tures" attract market systems of belief, and investments are made in a particular nation-state to the degree that one believes in its future. This novel, historical situation, of course, makes the nation-state unowned and ungovernable within its own borders, and, not surprisingly, mystery schools of economic patriotism, led by such figures as Congressman Richard Gephardt, arise to attempt to halt the planetary integration of all national economies.

The nation-state, however, will neither gain control of its destiny nor disappear, for in this process of "Symbiosis and Cell Evolution" nothing ever disappears; rather its forces of rejection are stabilized in a process whereby the very assertion of sovereignty and individuality creates the very energy that is used by the larger, invisible, and surrounding system to carry on its own larger business. National defense and national styles in music and fashion become exportable items: Israel now sells more arms than oranges and Britain exports its music, punk fashions, and its history as television specials for the new electronic global market. Arms races create associations between great power enemies, and local, contained wars are accepted by them as good for the arms business. Electronic forms of communication keep energizing differences at the very same time that they make the world smaller. Television doesn't eliminate local languages; in fact, its multichannel narrowcasting encourages the retention of vernacular languages and cultures, even within the United States. Where American mass culture once was widely spread, it is now breaking up into new subcultures.

Nothing disappears: you can find hunting bands in urban gangs, matrilineal society in rural communes and feminist mystery schools, civilization in the walled city-states of universities, and nation-states as investment opportunities for the global electronic economy pulsing through the planetary lattice of Tokyo–Hong Kong–Zürich–London–New York.

The presence of the past enables us to see that if nothing ever disappears, that the space of history is not a simple line from small to great, and from simple to complex. A human in a gathering and hunting band of 200,000 B.C. probably felt involved with a vast *umwelt* of heavenly bodies, landscapes, plants, and animals; and so sensitive and perceptive must have been the attention to this *umwelt* that it probably would dwarf the consciousness of the specialized and abstracted workers of today. Linear progressions tend to obscure the presence of the past. Prokaryotic bacteria have not gone away and, in spite of the Protestant Reformation, the medieval Catholic Church is still with us. If one part of the culture throws something away, you can be sure that another part of the culture will scavenge about and find another use for the object or activity as art. As Marshall McLuhan was fond of saying: "The sloughed-off environment becomes a work of art in the new and invisible environment." Spinning wheels become planters in suburban homes and welders become sculptors in an age of plastic.

Consider even McLuhan's ideas about the progression of the media of communication from script to print to electronic. If one lines up the five social forms of organization and their associated polities, one can see that the shift in social reorganization is also associated with a shift in the technology of communication.

I. Culture	I. Band	I. The Image
II. Society	II. Settlement	II. Pictographic
III. Civilization	III. City-State-Empire	III. Writing
IV. Industrialization	IV. Nation-State	IV. Print
V. Planetization	V. Biosphere	V. Electronic

In the movement from one social form to another, the old is not discarded, it is blessed and made holy or turned into a work of art. The paleolithic imagery from the walls of caves becomes more schematic as it is transferred to the walls of buildings and taken over by a new class of priestess specialists; and it becomes even more schematic as it is later transferred to designs for pottery or weavings. Ultimately the imagery can become so stylized that it can lose its meaning altogether. Few poker players today would recognize that the Joker is a transform of the image of the paleolithic shaman; that his floppy ears were originally an animal skin (such as is pictured in the cave painting of Trois Frères), that his phallic wand is a calendrical stick and the measure of time, and that his bells are testicles and show the old cosmology, discussed by Onians, in which one carried one's semen in one's head.

When writing takes over from pictographic imagery, the old is submerged in the new. The triangular icon of the vulva becomes the wedge-shaped stylus that is used to imprint onto the clay tablet. The Chinese ideogram becomes so stylized and transformed that its earlier form is no longer recognizable. When the printing of books takes over from scribal copying, then the loving labor of the hand does not disappear, it is transferred from vellum to canvas as the art of the landscape begins to give it more room than was allowed in the confines of the illuminated manuscript. And now in the shift from the printing of books and movies, videos are filled with quotes from old movies, false books are used as wall decoration by McDonald's fast-food restaurants in Paris, and the California chain of coffee shop-bookstores the Upstart Crow uses black-and-white photographs of popularly unrecognizable authors as wallpaper. In the space stations of the future, we will undoubtedly put ecosystems on the walls.

If we shift the focus of our attention from the means of communication to the polity, we can see that each shift in social form also brings with it a new obsessive concern. In the gathering and hunting band, the focus is on dominance and power. In tribal society, the concern is with authority. In civilization, with its conflicting mixture of tribes and technical specialists, the concern is with justice. In industrialization, with its impossibly large mixture of peoples, the concern is with representation. And now in Planetization, with its impossible mixtures of bands, tribes, city-states, peoples, and nations, the concern is with participation rather than representation.[8]

---

[8] For a lengthier discussion of this point, see W. I. Thompson, "Gaia and the Politics of Life" in *Gaia: A Way of Knowing, Political Implications of the New Biology* (Great Barrington, Mass.: Lindisfarne Press, 1987), p. 192.

I. Culture	I. Band	I. Dominance
II. Society	II. Tribe	II. Authority
III. Civilization	III. City-Empire	III. Justice
IV. Industrialization	IV. Nation	IV. Representation
V. Planetization	V. Biosphere	V. Participation

In each of these cases, it is precisely the means of communication that allows the focus of attention to dwell on the obsessive concern. Electronic media allow Greenpeace or the Palestinians to participate in the politics of France or Israel. Print allows pamphleteering and public pressure on gentlemen and ladies in Parliament who still seek to rule by the unwritten rules of the oral culture of their class. Writing allows laws to be written so that all can appeal to justice. And authority, whether it comes from Jahweh, Abraham, or Moses, is final and stops all the bickering between brothers, sisters, and wives. And behind the figure of authority, be she matriarch or be he patriarch, is the ultimate figure of the dominant primate, a figure that is still with us in gangs, corporations, universities, or dictatorships. Nothing ever disappears.

But novelty does appear, and it is in the process of emergence of novelty that the old continues its ancient ways in a new environment that can even be invisible to it. With the emergence of an oxygen atmosphere, the anaerobic bacteria take to the underworld of our guts or the bottom of lakes; they do not disappear from existence, merely from "the face of the earth." And so it is most likely to be with nation-states in the emergence of the biospheric politics of planetization. The increase in the ozone hole or the greenhouse effect will cause both nation-states and multinational corporations like Dupont to come into a new mental space they have not known before, and as these relationships are carried out, the seemingly nationalistic protests of the Palestinians, the Armenians, or the Basques will not cease. But if the Palestinians, the Kurds, the Armenians, the Corsicans, the Welsh, the Québecois were all to be granted national status by a global parliament overnight, the problem of being granted historical *representation* would not solve the present need for *participation* in the biospheric politics of the planet. Giving a flag to a nation-state, like giving a club jacket to a teenage gang, can help; the bestowal of identity, with its associated imaginative participation, can make the subways or the airlines safer, but it cannot deal with the postnational politics of the ozone hole or the greenhouse effect.

Industrialization threatens the destruction of the biosphere, and this new evil serves in the formation of the next political level of Planetization. Curious, isn't it? *Evil is the unconscious emergence of the next level of organization.* In a political situation of Dominance, Authority, whether it is the authority of the shaman or the midwife, is a threat to Power. In a situation of tribal authority, justice is a threat. (This situation is the subject of Aeschylus's *Oresteia* and Sophocles's *Antigone.*) In a situation of representation, participation is a threat to Power. The person who tries to seize participation is called a terrorist, even though the actual force applied by a France to a Greenpeace or by Israel to the Palestinians may be much greater, the use of force is always seen to be legitimate when used by the nation-state and illegitimate when used by the organelle within the polity of the biosphere.

Good and Evil, as the Buddhists would have it, do seem to be codependently defined in the interrelatedness of existence. In this complex dialectic in which nothing ever disappears but becomes enfolded in a new, and often invisible, envelopment, the tension of opposites seems to be one in which the very forces of repulsion create the energies of stitching the whole together. It is like death in Life. Stars explode in supernovae, and this seeds life for planets such as ours. What we unconsciously repel in visions of evil may actually be our future. As the Vedic sages described it: "We become what we hate." The abused child who hates its beater grows up to become a child-abuser; the Jews, the battered child of Europe, take on the

143

militarism of the Germans, and grow up to become Israelis who can now do to the Palestinians what the Germans did to them. This unconscious process of projection in human experience is what both the Hindus and the Buddhists call *karma*.

If evil is constituent of unconscious polities, then we should begin to suspect that we need to take a closer look at consciousness itself in history, and not always focus only on technology, the means of production, or even the means of communication. Is there a history of consciousness and could it be that there are mentalities as well that become incorporated in the process of symbiosis and cell evolution by which organelles are infolded within organisms?

Let us consider, for a moment, the terms Culture, Society, Civilization, Industrialization, and Planetization to refer not to the scale of size of social organizations and their extension in physical space, but, rather, to mentalities or world views.

Just what do we mean when we speak about the emergence of human culture? On the one side of this great divide, we imagine the animal, and on the other, the human. When I was an undergraduate, I was taught that it was technology that made us human, that animals didn't make tools. Never mind about otters, beavers, bees, and chimpanzees, this was a way of looking at things that was comfortable for a thingish, technological society. For a while, anthropologists thought it was language that made us human; then came the work of teaching Ameslan to chimpanzees, and now no one is too sure about that claim. Speech as we know it requires certain articulating capacities of the tongue and jaw, and physical anthropologists can show us with fossil skulls that this capacity became possible around 200,000 years ago. Since this is the time that decorated tools begin to appear, and since to chip away the part of a rock that isn't the tool one has to have in mind the logical set of "fist-hatchet" in order to make the member belong to the class, it is safe to say that there is an associated emergence, or general recursive system of feedback in the bringing forth of language and tools. The tool allows us to turn and transform our context to make the predator into the victim. The victim is the animal, the slayer is the human. And so literary anthropologists like Robert Ardrey or René Girard like to see the act of killing as the essential culture-creating act.[9]

Eros and Thanatos, however, have been with us since the eukaryotic cell, so focusing on hunting to the exclusion of gathering has given us too many male and egocentric narratives of prehistory, which the feminist anthropology of the last decade has worked to rewrite.

We back into an innovation by holding on to the past. We disguise a novel *structure* by filling it up with the past as a *content,* but in the very act of reducing a world to a mere content or quotation, we set up a larger and more obscure space in which we are looking back or down on the world that once was our entire reality. So if stone tools enable the human to slay the animal, spirituality enables him take on its skin in the costume of the shaman and art enables him to save the creature in the created image. There is not some primordial act of violence that once literally took place to make us human, once

---

[9] Robert Ardrey, *African Genesis* (New York: Dell, 1961). René Girard, *The Scapegoat* (Baltimore: Johns Hopkins University Press, 1985). At a conference on "Origins" at Stanford in 1987, Professor Girard talked about "the lie that is mythology," for he sees mythology as the camouflage that emerges to hide the act of murder that creates culture. He is quite literal, fundamentalist, and inflated in his presentation of the self, for he sees symbolism as a code that only he has cracked. Like many literary-code crackers, Freudian or otherwise, he tends to see the same story in all stories. As it turned out, the hidden agenda of the conference was to contribute to the apotheosis of Girard and to make up for the injustice of the fact that Derrida has wrongly taken the fame that Girard feels properly belongs to him. In the sociology of knowledge, the conference reduced all cultural history to the quarrel between two French intellectuals. A Girardian reading of "Rapunzel" would tell us that the Prince was originally killed by being thrown from the tower and that the meaning of the story is that the Prince is the scapegoat. Satisfied with having seen his obsession in the fairy tale, Girard would then move onto another tale, to show us the same story there. All the other levels and the fullness of meaning that I have tried to show in "Rapunzel" would not be possible in the tight training of Girardian literary exegesis. His is a very Catholic philosophy in which all pre-Christian mythologies are inadequate and murderous. It is a philosophy that describes itself, for mythology is the victim, and in killing it, he gives birth to the culture of his school.

and for all, as Freud and René Girard would have it; there is a linguistic and technological emergence in which unconscious and instinctive killing, the chemical cannibalism of one microbe by another or the eating of one animal by another, becomes conscious and articulated in image and sound, art and ritual. We call this emergent property, "Culture."

In the emergence of language and technology there arises a novel and contradictory tension between conscious and unconscious. Language and technology both work to heighten consciousness, so the way in which we humans back into the innovation is to work to reachieve unconsciousness in the context of consciousness by going into trance. The charismatic figure takes on the sloughed-off animal skin, reverses consciousness by going into trance, and becomes the Shaman. In the evolution of the human spirit, the mentality associated with Culture is Shamanism. Shamanism is a way of coming to terms with the contradictory tension between consciousness and the unconscious.

Unconscious<————(Trance)————>Conscious

One axiomatic way of expressing this contradictory tension between an innovating technology and a conserving art is to say that: *"We slay with technology and save the victim with art."* In Culture, the victim is the animal, the technology is that of stone tools and engraved imagery, the spiritual complex is shamanism, and the focus of identity is on blood: the blood of the victim, the numinous menstrual blood that covers the ochre-stained Great Mother of Laussel, the blood that unites the small, intimately related group.

I. CULTURE

Victim: the Animal

Complex: Shamanism

Technology: Stone tools and engraved imagery

Mode of Identity: Sanguinal

Mode of Consciousness: Trance

Archetypal Examples: Laussel, Lascaux, Trois Frères

At the level of human culture in gathering and hunting, there is no fixed settlement and no accumulation of private property; there is a seasonal round and a balance between the activities of the male in hunting and fishing and the activities of the female in gathering, but in the evolution of culture into society, the complexification of the scale and the diversity of human activities creates a new distance between the activities of the male and the female. As the gathering of the women becomes increasingly effective in producing food, the technology of grinding seeds into meal and of storing food makes the nodal point of female activity more of a fixed settlement, a secure point around which the women can gather seeds, fruits, nuts, roots, and tubers and a center around which the men can range even further for hunting and fishing. As the compost heap of gathering begins to sprout into first the accidental garden, and then the consciously planted one, the storage of food begins to accumulate a new technology of heavy stones for grinding, lunar sickles with flints for gathering wild grasses, then clay for storage, and finally ovens for baked pottery and bread. Women in their traditional role of gathering, with the infant in a sling over their hips and the food in a sack over their shoulders, begin to concentrate on the activities of a single area and it becomes harder for them to pack up an entire settlement. It is easier for the men to go off on a hunting or fishing party and to bring back the food that is flashy, festive, and highly perishable. The activity of the male, an activity that is both spiritual, economic, and sexual, is a phallic activity of the instantaneous and vanishing mode of time. The erection of Eros, as well as the fresh meat of the kill of Thanatos,

147

both can be fulfilling, but short-lived. The all-containing power of the female in breast and clay pot, womb and infant sling, gathering sack for seeds and vagina, is the complementary opposite: she is the fixed and enduring mode of time. Already from the earliest human high art in the Pleistocene, we can begin to trace the lineaments of a cosmology in which the male principle is short-lived, tragic, and vanishing, and the female principle is stable and enduring. Michaelangelo's dead Christ in the arms of Mary, the *Pietá,* is an archetypal expression precisely because as a work of art it plays upon cosmological imagery that goes back to the very origins of European art in the scene from the pit at Lascaux.[10] This cosmology in which the male principle is the dynamic and the female is the static has its roots in Magdalenian, paleolithic art and culture, and it became archetypal simply because the cultural changes brought about by mesolithic and neolithic societies served to intensify it. Mesolithic culture added the discovery of the bow and arrow to the tool kit of the male hunt, so the short and intense flight of the arrow became male and phallic, whereas the curved body of the bow could be seen as female and lunar and was, not surprisingly, later taken over in the iconography of the Amazons and the goddess Diana. The bow and arrow enable the male to hunt in the forest and to range farther from the fixed point of the settlement; it also enables the hunting band to become the raiding party, so that another band's fixed property of grains and grinding stones can become objects for seizure. And as women become increasingly fixed to the earth in the growing complexification of gathering into gardening, they, too, became objects for plunder.

It takes a long time for gathering to evolve into gardening

---

[10] I have discussed this cosmology, in relation to the theories of the prehistorian André Leroi-Gourhan, at greater length in *The Time Falling Bodies Take to Light: Mythology, Sexuality, and the Origins of Culture* (New York: St. Martin's Press, 1981), pp. 102–130.

for the females, and it takes a long time for hunting to evolve into animal husbandry. As men begin to hold their animals in boxed canyons with a barricade at one end, it begins to become possible to think of building a barricade into a corral or to follow the movement of the animals up to high ground with the retreat of the snow in springtime. As the men begin to live in seasonal encampments and to keep animals and not simply to kill them opportunistically, they can begin to observe their habits and the inheritance of traits in breeding. Thus, over the millennia, two very different ways of life begin to evolve. There is the settled way of life of gathering, gardening, and, finally, agriculture; and there is the nomadic way of life in hunting, fishing, herding, and, finally, the stock breeding of cattle and sheep. Around one way of life we have the figure of traditional authority of the Matriarch, a figure that, because it antedates literature, is only remembered in her iconic form as the Great Mother. And around the other we have the figure of the Patriarch, a biblical Father Abraham with his herds. Stock breeding and paternity are activities that bring forth a consciousness and a culture of fathers and sons, of the inheritance of property. But the earlier culture, the culture of paleolithic Dolne Vestonice and neolithic Çatal Hüyük, is the matrilineal one in which the mother is the source of nourishment, the source of the economy, the source of children, the source of identity, the source of life.

With a population in the thousands, what we see in Çatal Hüyük is a neolithic metropolis in which the old cosmology is articulated into priestcraft. The Great Mother sits on her leopard throne and is attended by priests in leopard skins. The statue of the young male god is buried with the old crone in the vulture shrine of death. And on the walls are paintings of the animals in a chase that has become a highly stylized ritual quest, with dancers and musicians performing as the animals are caught with ropes. The chase has now become a content in a new structure, a structure of high technological inventiveness that includes copper metalurgy and the polishing of obsidian mirrors. The ritual animal of the chase is no longer the economic source of life on which this agricultural town depends, for the volcanic breasts of the Great Mother produce the dark obsidian that is the source of wealth for trade and the fields produce the food surplus that is the source for the expanding population. The animal of the hunt becomes the meat of sacrifice and ritual, and the male is buried in the corner of the dwelling with his old paleolithic tools, but the female is buried in the center with all the costly jewelry and new riches of neolithic culture. Here, there is no great Man the Hunter or Father Abraham the Patriarch; the male is no hero, but a compliant figure whose time is short and whose space is contained by the majesty of the Great Mother.

In the emergence of Culture, the animal was the victim, slain with technology and saved with art. In the emergence of Society in agricultural Çatal Hüyük, Man is the victim, slain with technology and saved with art. He is the male who takes his body in birth from the female, who takes his nourishment for a time from her breast, but who must give back, "according to Necessity and the arrangement of Time," his semen to her womb and his body to her earth. As we move forward in time in a process of increasing individuation, it is no longer a case of the Shaman surrendering for a time his consciousness in the seizure of trance; it is the sacrificial offering in which the male must give his body to fertilize the earth. For tens of thousands of years in Pleistocene art, the male principle had been the vanishing one, but now in agricultural society, the male becomes the dying corn god of the year, a figure we can see sculpted in Çatal Hüyük and whose story we can read in the tragic rise and fall of Dumuzi in Sumerian mythology.

II. SOCIETY

Victim: Man

Complex: Matriarchy

Technology: Agriculture and Iconography

Mode of identity: Territorial

Mode of Consciousness:

Dismemberment<———(Sacrifice) ———>Incarnation

Archetypal Examples: Hacilar and Çatal Hüyük

For several thousand years, this complex is stable and enduring, but, as with all things, its strength is its weakness and tragic flaw. The source of wealth for Çatal Hüyük was obsidian, and we can trace the lattice work of traded implements all the way down from Anatolia into Palestine. As trade begins to create a lattice of activity far beyond the fixed settlement, the old archetypal patterns of the male in the seasonal round and in the hunt can turn on the spiral and reincarnate themselves in new flesh. Male bonding can reassert itself in trading and raiding parties, and the assertion into new space can carry seeds of many cultures and other worlds. The Great Mother sits on her throne: enormous and conservative are her ways; she does not change. But the male, tragic or not, is dynamic, changing, risk taking, and extrovertedly adventurous as he looks for value, not in the retaining and conservative mode of Being, but in the quest, that search for adventure and meaning in new spaces in the company of beings. As trade begins to produce its own economic surplus, and as raiding begins to develop into seriously sustained invasions, the lattice work of neolithic Society begins to extend far beyond the settlement of the town. The town simply becomes the nucleus sustained by a cytoplasm of much more extensive space. Precisely as this space expands, the town compacts to become the defensively walled city.

With the urban revolution of the fourth millennium B.C., neolithic society becomes the content in the new structure of Civilization. Gardening becomes irrigation agriculture with its vastly expanded new technologies of oxen and plows (the male and his animals), dikes and ditches (the female with her vulva) under the control and prosperous management of the seminal waters of Enki. Writing and standing armies become the new innovations as the sword, the plow, and the stylus impress into the soft and submissive earth and clay, the new forces of the male. To disguise this innovation, humans, as always, even with the illusory conservatism of Ronald Reagan, back into the radically new by making the past the content of their attention in a structure that is beyond anything known in the past.

In patriarchal Civilization, Woman is the Victim. Matriarchy is miniaturized and transformed into the household, and the old cosmology is miniaturized and transformed into the new complex of Religion. Male scribes with their phallic styli take on the iconic power of the vulva in *cuneiform*; they wear priestly garments that recall the old ways of women sages, and the male leaders take the calendrical stick of the midwife and transform it into the scepter and the *baton de commandement*. In the war of the sexes, that cosmological battle of vanishing and permanence, it is now the male's turn. The ways of custom and traditional authority, the ways of blood and the blood mysteries of the furies are transformed by written laws and male solar gods into the law courts of the city-state. The Great Mother, be she Tiamat or Clytaemnestra, is murdered and from her torn body the new state, be it Babylon or Athens, is constructed.

As traditional customs give way to written laws and mythologies, the very codification of the mythology into literature creates a new canonical doctrine stored in the temples by priests. A whole system of belief in written doctrine is brought forth, and a new act of belief is called for. The illiterate must assent to the written doctrine of the literate priesthood. But the very act of calling for submission, paradoxically, affirms the value of the one who must comply, and a linguistic domain of common speech and a common doctrine for the polity creates a new system of identity and identification in which the individual is brought forth. The individual ego is separated out and heightened in consciousness by the very process in which consciousness is separated and set forth in literacy. In Belief, one is affiliated and affirmed in relationship to the linguistic domain of the community; outside the language, one is alone and separated.

In the emergence of human *Culture*, consciousness was affirmed by returning it in unconsciousness in trance; in *Society*, the individual was affirmed by giving back the body of his individuality in sacrifice; now in *Civilization*, the individual is affirmed by being constrained to give back his individuality through belief in the common doctrine.

III. CIVILIZATION

Victim: Woman

Complex: Religion

Technology: Writing, Irrigation, and Militarism

Mode of Identity: Linguistic

Mode of Consciousness:

  Belief in Doctrine<———(Faith)———>Individuated Ego

Literary Examples: the *Oresteia,* and the *Enuma Elish*

For thousands of years, Civilization was the rule, and from China through India to Europe and across to the civilizations of the Americas, the cultures were urban, male, literate, agricultural, and militaristic. They were all hierarchical and run by classes of knights and priests. And then, around the pivotal point of 1500, something new began to emerge. And once again, as it was in the case of Çatal Hüyük in 6500 B.C., it was the extended latticework of trade that challenged the settled forms of authority in the landed rulers and priests. The linguistic domain of a common system of belief breaks up as traders learn many languages and know many gods; the individual in this context of a vastly extended and open space is able to doubt, to hesitate, or choose to which system of belief to give assent.

Skepticism, doubt, and even cynicism, of course, were known before 1500, but the Roman response to the diversity of cultures, languages, and religions was an attempt to create a civic religion and give rights to the citizen in return for compliance to a lip service to the imperial formalities. Christians, with their insistence on an absolutistic religion, were a nuisance, for they took Faith beyond any measure known before. So extreme were their beliefs that they no longer belonged to any community on earth. As the medieval church institutionalized this system of belief in doctrine and consolidated it into the very language of the oppressor, Latin, the centrality of the world was organized around Rome in the new imperium of the Church. But as Venice, and Florence, and Genoa extended their own trading empires, the concentric world broke apart into a much more complex and polycentric topology of a world economy and not a world empire with a single center and a bounded periphery. Priests and knights are bound up in their tradition-bound identities, but capitalists can trade with infidels and do business with enemies.

The demand for belief, paradoxically, affirmed the value of the individual mind, and one had only to hesitate or doubt to reaffirm the value of an individual, alone, but adequate in his aloneness. As Milton framed it, unconsciously seeing evil as the emergence of the next level of organization, and therefore putting the words into the mouth of Satan: "The mind is its own place, and in itself, can make a Hell of Heaven, a Heaven of Hell."

As people began to feel the strain of the emergence of an entirely new mentality, madness began to become the focus of attention and the great works of Shakespeare's *King Lear* and Cervantes's *Don Quixote* are milestones in the history of consciousness. In this new mentality, the motion of falling bodies became the focus of attention, and the individual as a body fallen away from the Church was on the move into a state of sin and a new society. The very story of his sins became fascinating and autobiography became a new literary genre of the movement from rags to riches in the bourgeois world of Capitalism.

In this New World, it was no longer a question of believing, but knowing, and artists and scientists in their new ways of knowing the world succeed in taking charisma away from Holy Mother Church. The individual, archetypally celebrated in the charismatic function of the individual genius, a Leonardo, a Michaelangelo, a Galileo, a Newton, or a Descartes, now became the wedge for the expansion of the middle classes. Religion and feudal civilization became the victim. From Renaissance painting in Italy to the industrial Crystal Palace in London, or from Raphael to the Pre-Raphaelites, Religion becomes the visible content of the invisible structure; religion is the victim that is slain by technology and saved by art.

IV. INDUSTRIALIZATION

Victim: Religion

Complex: Art and Science

Technology: Print and Mechanization

Mode of Identity: Material objects, possessions

Mode of Consciousness:

Collective Knowledge<———(Knowing)———>the Genius

Archetypal Example: Descartes

The new philosophy called all in doubt; it split the world into the objective world of machines and the subjective world of feelings, the public world of the middle classes expressed in new collective forms of banking systems, libraries, and universities, and the private world of the bourgeois individual in his book-lined study, filled with aesthetic sensations and angst-ridden thoughts. This rise of the individual is, however, linked to the expansion of mass society, first to the expansion of the entrepreneurial class in industrial society, then of the consuming class in postindustrial society. Science, art, and technology take over the power and authority of the Church, but science is as paradoxical as Shamanism, for it celebrates the individual genius, and yet it is essentially a collective activity that requires bureaucracies and strict conformity to the various scientific thought collectives.

In the evolution of consciousness from Shamanism to Religion to Art and Science, the role of evil is critical. Evil is a form of unconscious emergence that brings forth a new world that is then transformed into the Good. Godhead may be One, but "as the one becomes two," contradiction enters the world of consciousness, and the demiurge has two faces, or is a twin of Christ and the Devil. Recall that the first projection outward of Atlantic European civilization was the Viking Terror that attacked the foundations of Christendom in sacking the monasteries; centuries later when European, industrial civilization had moved from its waves of succession to a climax civilization, it still took two world wars to sublimate the pagan gods into the bourgeois, parliamentary, liberal democracies of Bonn, London, and Washington.

But all throughout history this painful and suffering condition of *samsara* has been the ground of the human formation of consciousness. If one cannot go into trance and take on the mind of the animal spirit, one is not as "good" as the shaman. But if one looks at the fully socialized person from another perspective, then the fully individuated consciousness, one cut off from the old collective consciousness of nature, is not evil, but is prophetic of the cultural evolution to come. The civilized person may be closed to possession by trance by gods or the elemental spirits of nature, but he or she is open to take on doctrines and systems of conscious beliefs. If, however, one cannot believe, then he or she, from the point of view of the civilized priesthood, is sinful. And yet the sinful person that is outside the civilized system of belief can begin to question and explore the world through knowing. The transition from one mentality to another is not a simple accretive process of the increase of facts, opinions, and ideas; it is a transformative process in which the basic grammar, with its implicit world view that rules all the words, is changed.[11] When an individual goes through such a metanoia as an adult and parts company from the mentality of his companions, whether the companions are Catholics or Communists, this change is seen to be so profoundly threatening that the person is seen to have fallen from grace.

I. Culture: shamanism
Unconscious<————(Trance)————>Conscious

II. Society: matriarchy
Dismemberment<————(Sacrifice)————>Incarnation

III. Civilization: religion
Belief in doctrine<————(Faith)————>Individuation

IV. Industrialization: art & science
Collective Knowledge<————(Knowing)————>Solitary
Genius

As in the turning of a DNA helix, the movement through this historical structure is not a simple one in which the Left side of the chart is bad and the Right side good. "Dismember-

---

[11] I have discussed the relationship between mathematical modes of world description and literary forms of narrative in *Pacific Shift* (San Francisco: Sierra Club Books, 1986), pp. 93–144, so I shall not repeat the argument here, but it does serve as the foundation for this subsequent discussion.

ment" can be seen as birth, a tearing away from the womb; death can be seen as a rememberment in which the individual returns to the source of life. And the peculiarly long-lived quality of these archetypal patterns can often create an "impure" condition in which an earlier process affects the manner or tonality in which a novel activity is performed. Sacrifice can become an ecstatic trance, faith can become a sacrifice of one's mind, and heretical knowers can become martyrs to the cause of Science. Indeed, the ambiguity of conscious individuation has often fascinated romantic artists such as Rilke or thinkers such as Nietzsche, for the seductive pull of the feminine into the Eternal Round is compelling to them, and it is small wonder that Lou Andreas-Salomé was photographed with whip in hand as Nietzsche and Paul Reé were yoked to her wagon.[12] For the romantic mind, there is a fascination in the pull of the Eternal Return to "the eternal feminine which draws us on," as Goethe phrased it.

If the structure of consciousness in the individual is a contradictory tension stretched between unconsciousness and consciousness, total envelopment and total alienation, the shape of this field should not be seen as that of a simple dipolar magnetic field that moves through history with new iron filings added as facts and opinions, such that a woman in 6000 B.C. and a man in 1500 A.D. have the same mind filled up with different facts. The morphology itself of this mind is changing. If we take Ralph Abraham's theories of Chaos Dynamics and superimpose them over my narrative of the progression from Culture to Society to Civilization to Industrialization, then we can see a moiré pattern emerge in which the changes of mentality can be described as changes in *attractors*.[13]

The mentality for "Culture" is a *static attractor*, and unconsciousness "consists of a single state, at which the system comes

---

[12] See H. F. Peters, *My Sister, My Spouse: A Biography of Lou Andreas-Salomé* (New York: Norton, 1974), p. 155.

[13] Ralph Abraham, "Mathematics and Evolution: A Manifesto" in *IS Journal* 1 (Los Angeles: December 1986), p. 17.

to rest." Unconsciousness and the Great Mother are the basin to which the system returns and comes to rest. "Society" and "Civilization" are expressions of a *periodic attractor,* "a cycle of states repeated again and again." The male is born, flourishes for a season, then dies and returns to the Mother. The statue of the male in the vulture shrine at Çatal Hüyük and Michaelangelo's dead Christ in the arms of Mary, the *Pietá,* are archetypal images that repeat the pattern in which the Great Mother is the "basin" that pulls the individually existent entity back to its primal condition, then gives birth to another male, to repeat the cycle over and over again. "Industrialization" is a *chaotic attractor.* "The long-run behavior is neither settling to rest, nor is it approximately periodic." The turbulence of such a dynamical system is far more complex than the classical city-world empire in which there is a center and a periphery. In the shift from the medieval world *ecclesia* centered in Rome to a world economy, the field of human activity became so complexly polycentric that the old mentality of construing the world became inadequate, and so the mathematics of the period shifted. In the Platonic scheme of things, the heavens are concentric, and motion is neatly idealized in a periodic fashion in the "saving of the appearances." Motion is considered fallen, the impure world of time, and not the pure world of eternity. Obviously, the condition of ideal grace here is the static attractor, the return to the timeless. So archetypally compelling is this pull that even today, intellectuals in the "New Age" movement of a Neoplatonic persuasion, British intellectuals such as Kathleen Raine and Keith Critchlow, see change as a threat to the unchanging values of eternity, and my metanoia away from this way of looking at "art and the sacred" was, typically, indeed archetypically, seen as a fall into the profane.[14] Conservative thinkers have always recoiled

---

[14] In this sense, this book, as well as my fictional work, *Islands Out of Time,* can be read as expressions of a metanoia, a shift from the rigid and reactionary values of a medieval geometry and its New Age mystery school that I had helped to support, to the moving geometries of life and science explored here.

from the turbulent flow of culture and nature in "Industrialization," and Heidegger's discussion of being in his *Introduction to Metaphysics*,[15] in which physis is seen as the arising and setting up from a more primordial Being, should be seen as the work of a mentality drawn back to the archetypal patterns of consciousness, not of civilization, but farther back to matrilineal Society itself. Although Heidegger praised poetry as a form of expression, his writing is too disembodied and abstract, for his setting up and arising of physis is the unrecognized phallic cosmology of neolithic society, and his Being is the Great Mother. Following Anaximander, he demythologizes the mentality of prehistory, and then laments his alienation and succumbs to the seduction of counterfeit mythologies in Nazism. The chaos dynamics of "Industrialization," of course, disturb more than the twentieth-century spokepersons for German Romanticism or the British Neoplatonic tradition, and many of the Greens of the radical Left in Europe and America also long for a prehistoric mentality, "a return to nature" in an ideal ecological society in which the turbulence of the system with its intolerable conditions of pollution and noise can finally come to rest. Some ecologists, such as Edward Goldsmith in Britain, Arne Naes in Norway, and Rudolph Bahro in Germany, envision this in preindustrial terms in a form of neofeudalism.[16] When contrasted to the ugliness of a modern city like Frankfurt or Mexico City, such visions of a return to nature are very compelling, but were we to achieve them, we probably would find them to be as intellectually asphyxiating as the air in Athens or Los Angeles.

If "evil" has been part of a process of bifurcation in which the "phase portraits" of various mentalities have gone through

---

[15] See Martin Heidegger, *An Introduction to Metaphysics* (New Haven, Conn.: Yale University Press, 1980), p. 71.

[16] To get a sense of this sensibility, one should peruse numerous copies of the British journals, *Resurgence,* edited by Satish Kumar, and *The Ecologist,* edited by Edward Goldsmith, both published in Devon, England.

transformations as we have moved from Culture to Society, or from Society to Civilization, then, perhaps, we should begin to suspect that noise, pollution, and "evil" are now also constitutive of some larger process of the phase portrait of our emergent planetary culture. In the bifurcation between Industrialization and Planetization, there is a great divide between those who hold the traditional Renaissance mentality we have had since the emergence of modernism, and those who express the emergent properties of a mentality that is planetary. Whether this bifurcation will be one of the three major kinds in chaos dynamics, namely, "subtle, explosive, or catastrophic," is not yet clear.

Personally, I feel that chaos dynamics has become articulated at this time because we are at the end of a cultural epoch and it expresses the sunset effect of the dynamical mentality of modernism and Industrialization. The planetary dynamics of the Gaia hypothesis would seem to me to express a meta-system, a processual morphology, in which chaos-dynamics randomize conditions to generate the possibilities, the changes of state, that we call evolution. However, these eddies of chaos in a turbulent flow seem to resolve into a more complex, multidimensional morphology, one for which we have no name at the moment, since we are at the very beginning of the emergence of this planetary mentality. I have focused on the process of the assembly of the organelles in the evolution of the eukaryotic cell in Lynn Margulis's work, on the atmospheric chemistry of Lovelock's work, and the cognitive domains of the immune system in Varela's work, because I have an Irish hunch that these three different cognitive domains are the places in which the processual morphologies of the future will enact these behaviors in new mythic, literary, and scientific narratives. And one of the characteristics that I think these morphologies and narratives will have is a new form of a vision of the ancient Buddhist concept of "codependent origination" in which good and evil are involved in a larger process that cannot be mapped in a simple, ideological fashion of good guys versus bad guys. Rather than generating the nihilism and immorality that moralists fear, this new planetary mentality could actually generate the compassion for symbionts in history that could teach English and Irish, Israeli and Palestinian, black and white, how to coevolve.

If evil has in the past been characteristic of the bifurcations that have expressed the phase portraits of cultural systems, then perhaps we need to take a closer look at our fears and terrors of the moment as a way of trying to feel our way through the darkness of our contemporary historical condition.

We are certainly afraid of war, of pollution that can damage or destroy the biosphere, and we are also afraid of the young and fear that civilization, literacy, and morality are being swamped in some punk apocalypse of noise and cultural entropy. We read in the newspaper stories of how youth gangs in Los Angeles initiate members into their groups by requiring the aspirant to shoot a child, swinging in a playground, or on the steps of his home; we read stories of how the soldiers in Ceylon shot a nursing mother and shot off the toes of the baby for target practice, or of how the Shiites in the Soviet Union ripped open the womb of a pregnant Armenian woman and tore the limbs from the fetus, and we know that no moral vision of horror of apocalyptic artists such as Anthony Burgess and Doris Lessing is equal to the terror of the daily news. "What the hell is going on?" we ask ourselves, and we know that it is precisely hell that is going on.

In response to these literally chaotic cultural events, it is small wonder that minds recoil and seek a condition of rest in totalitarian, fundamentalist explanations; and yet the very proliferation of hysterical fundamentalisms, Christian, Shiite, or Sikh, does not seem to generate compassion, but the very opposite: it grants the true believer a license to kill, and the chaos goes into a runaway condition.

So we have to find another way to look at the imaginary landscape of our contemporary historical condition, and my role in this mind-jazz session with Abraham, Lovelock, Margulis, and Varela has been to work to bring forth the historical and cultural pattern of which we are all a part, to try to write a description of planetary culture that is itself a performance of the very reality it seeks to describe.

What does the world look like when one looks out through the enactive embodiment of this new culture of nature? First of all, karma becomes seen as the generation of unconscious polities in which we do not take responsibility for our own affirmations through negation.[17] We become what we hate and we generate shadow economies, such as the drug economy in the United States, that are caricatures of the conscious economy. We cannot naively work to eliminate a General Noriega of Panama if we cannot see how a Latin American strongman is a cultural hero who is taking revenge for the "development" of the Third World by the banks of the United States, for our exports to them are as polluting as their exports to us, but their exports are a much more honest and less hypocritical expression of the damage to cultures and ecologies.

Second, the arms race between the United States and the U.S.S.R. becomes seen as an unconscious form of planetization that needs to be sublimated into a process of more Stars and less War, for if the shift to a scientific economy from a consumers' postindustrial economy is to be accomplished in a more enlightened fashion in which industrial pollution can be transformed from an unconscious dumping to an affirmed and accepted microbial culture. In this shift to a global scientific economy, the arms race between the Soviet Union and the United States is being phased out as these enemies begin to recognize that they are mirror images of one another, for the American annexation of Texas, California, Hawaii, and the Philippines is not unlike the Soviet annexations of Estonia or Afghanistan.

---

[17] See "Gaia and the Politics of Life," p. 167, op. cit.

History is rarely a happy place, so there is always the danger that the end of the Cold War could bring a racial convergence in which a new European civilization proposed to the Russians by Gore Vidal, one that stretches westward from Vladivostok to Vancouver, will try to stand off "the yellow peril" of a rich Japan and a prodigious China. If the cultural bifurcation of the world continues along these lines, then zones of cultural entropy in Africa, the Middle East, and Latin America, will so terrify entities such as Israel and South Africa that they will never surrender to forces of liberal tolerance but will become entrenched, technological fortresses in which the Great White Race makes its last stand.

But persuaded by my years of living in Toronto and partaking of the insights of the Torontonian school of Innis and McLuhan, I do not think that the formations of nineteenth-century empires can now reassert themselves, for they were built on print, bureaucracies, and the center-periphery dynamics of railways and shipping lines. In a global ecology of mind that is polycentric and electronic, I think that the nativistic movements of premodernist Islam and modernist Europe are both bound to fail, just as the Ghost Dance and Louis Riel's rising of the Métis failed in North America. Precisely in order to avoid a world organized along lines of racial hatred, my allegiances are to such universal forms of human association as are expressed in Varela's Western science and Eastern Buddhism.

Third, in this perspective of planetary culture, the "noise" of the popular culture of the young must be accepted and seen as expressing an emergent property in which noise is the solvent of the individuality characteristic of modernism. If we slay with technology and save the victim with art, then in Planetization, the "mind" is the victim.

V. PLANETIZATION

Victim: the Mind

Complex: Music

Technology: Electronics

Mode of Identity: Planetary

Mode of Consciousness:

Noise<————(Participation)———— >Rapture

Archetypal Examples: heavy metal, Musak in shopping malls, hotels, and elevators, and especially the role of Muzak at Epcot and Disney World.

Noise is disintegration of the signal, an information overload in which sanity and tranquility can become impossible. This condition can generate paranoia, or simply a catatonic shutdown of perception. Rapture (and here I have consciously chosen the word used by the Christian fundamentalists to describe the end of the world when two are working in the field together, but only one of the faithful is taken up), is also the word we use to suggest exalted and ecstatic knowing: the spirit of the cognitive bliss of Varela's dream in which he heard the music of creation as he watched the dancing spheres of the bacteria in Lynn Margulis's film. This form of the exaltation of knowing into cognitive bliss expresses the apotheosis of the individual and for me always brings to mind the *Sanctus* of Bach's B Minor Mass.

Mere listening can be passive, but participation is enactive and it requires one's body to be entirely there, and so, for the young, the gatherings at rock concerts is an important participation in their evolutionary dance of being part of a historical emergence. Participation is an atunement (to use a favorite word at the New Age spiritual community of Find-

horn in Scotland) in which the flesh turns to crystal in a planetary lattice of sound and light. But this vision of the end of
"man" can also be seen as a vision of evil in which the flesh is,
after the fashion of the sci-fi illustrations of *Omni* magazine, or
bad movies such as *The Quatermas Conclusion*, or brilliant films
such as David Cronenberg's *Videodrome*, embedded in the
vibrating media whose pulsations alter the body to bring forth
a demonic world. In Cronenberg's disturbing study of his fellow Torontonian Marshall McLuhan, the Noosphere of Chardin and McLuhan's Catholic vision of the Mystical Body of
Christ,[18] become a Satanic collectivization, not a release from
matter but a gnostic entrapment in a planetary electronic network.

If we are experiencing the emergence of a new mentality,
then it is not surprising that both visions of good and evil can
outline its form. And if this form is also a new mode of narration in mathematics and myth, then we will not be able to understand the processual morphology of the future if we seek
to model it as an oscillating, periodic attractor of good guys
versus bad guys. The traditional mythological system of the
battle of Christ and Satan in history must needs be seen in a
new way. Rudolph Steiner articulated a Christology in which
Christ is the human mediation between the demonic Ahriman
and the satanic Lucifer. Ahriman is the unit crushed into the
uniform, the destruction of individuality in sameness.
Ahriman is the spirit behind Stalin, or Orwell's nightmares of
Big Brother. Lucifer is the opposite, the individual raised, in
the unbounded pride of the sin of *superbia*, to a cosmic ego-
tism in which there can be no other one, not even God. The
Ahrimanic evil is the state that crushes all diversity; it is the
war-time economy of an Iraq and an Iran in which all life, all
art, all science, and all sensuous happiness must be sacrificed
to the Moloch of battle. The Luciferic evil is the overweening

---

[18] See Marshall McLuhan's interview in *Playboy*, March 1969.

pride of the scientist who believes he can do better by taking over the control of evolution through the genetic engineering of life in his laboratory. The Christ, however, is neither the unit and the uniform, nor the alone, but expresses the crossing of the unique and the universal.

Ahriman<————(Christ)————>Lucifer

The popular music of the young seems to express all the contradictions of our contemporary consciousness, writ large on a global scale. On the one hand, pop music is the apotheosis of the individual, the individual as rock star; but, on a closer look, these individuals could be anybody. They are packaged and produced by a manufacturing process, and neither genius nor talent is necessarily required. In fact, the ordinariness of a Tiffany seems to be part of her appeal to teenage audiences, for it allows a *participation mystique* to stimulate the fantasies on which the whole musical economy runs. One is not interested in voting for Prince and sending him as a representative to Congress, but in the mentality shift from *representation* to *participation* that is characteristic of Planetization, one is interested in being part of the music of what is happening.

If we consider Steiner's biospheric vision of humanity in which the prokaryotic cell is one chapter in the evolution of the human body, then we also have to consider that this hominid moment that we too restrictingly identify as "us" may also be one chapter, and that what our beatific visions of heaven and our terrifying visions of hell may be all about are descriptions of an evolutionary crisis, or catastrophe-bifurcation, that paranoids call "the end of the world." David Cronenberg's *Videodrome* is an artistic form of a paranoid narrative in which a videotape is literally able to change the nervous system, but paranoid narratives do have a way of caricaturing and rendering visible a process that is occurring outside the perceptions of normalcy or a dominant historical mentality. It was not the end of the world in 1500, although Bosch painted *The Last Judgment*, and it may not be the end of the world now, but merely a catastrophic bifurcation in which a new attractor, a new world system with a new mentality, appears out of the blue. The "Rapture" may not be the literal nuclear war that the fundamentalists are looking forward to; it may be an increasingly electronic landscape, from manufactured viruses to artificial intelligence in satellite networks, in which humans become the visible content in the invisible structure. If pop music and planetary happenings like Woodstock and Africa Live Aid are foreshadowings of the musical polities of the future, then "nature" and "culture" will not be what either the Greens or the industrialists of today imagine. As vibratory music transforms culture into a new nature, the landscape in which the individual dwells will also be radically transformed. Since the processual morphologies of the mentality I am referring to are not yet historically on my perceptual horizon, I am forced to guess and imagine.

In Culture the ego was diffuse; in Society the ego became articulated and defined in the mystery school of death; in Civilization the ego became discrete, a literately defined center with a sharply defined periphery; in Industrialization the ego became a turbulent flow, a chaotic attractor with the power of a Cosimo di Medici, a Descartes, a Beethoven, and a Napoleon to break through boundaries and definitions to amass the glory, and power, and wealth that it felt was its proper destiny; now in Planetization the ego is no longer diffuse, certainly no longer articulate, unable any longer to be discrete in the privacy of its civilized study, and no longer able to expect the biosphere to sustain the amassing of its glory and wealth. The *diachronic* flow of the ego has come to its end, and now the *synchronic* dimensions of the spiritual Daimon is beginning to infold itself into temporal consciousness. Multidimensionality begins to be experienced as the personal field of consciousness, the interrelatedness of all sentient beings in "the innumerable universes that are suspended from the tip of

Buddha's hair." Lacking the appropriate and futuristic image to "imagine" this, so very much like a cultural historian, I fall back upon the past and envision the Sephiroth, the Tree of Life from the Judaic Kabbalah, but I see this flat rendering on a two-dimensional page transformed into a multidimensional crystal in which the lattice is a recursive one in which the "ego" is the foundation, but all the other nodes are also part of the architecture of an individual, but enlightened consciousness.

Between the angelic heights of the macrocosm of the Gaian atmosphere and the elemental depths of the microcosm of the bacterial earth lies the middle way of the Mind, and it is in this imaginary landscape of the middle way, whether we call it the Madhyamika of Buddhism or the Christ of Steiner or the *Da át* of the Kabbalah,[19] that we humans take our life and come to know our world as the dark horizon that illuminates our hidden center.

---

[19] See Gershom Scholem, *Kabbalah* (New York: New American Library, 1978), p. 107.

GAIAN COSMOLOGIES:
A Cycle of Poems
for Four Friends

I. INTERCEPTIONS OF STARLIGHT

(For Francisco)

Alone in the Sangre de Cristo mountains at night,
Asleep in the angular stone tower, you hear
Unearthly music and wake without dreams
To see, framed in the skylight above the bed,
High at their autumn zenith, the Pleiades.
For a moment you think you feel you have knowledge
Of other worlds and while the subtle body,
Struck by starlight like crystal still rings,
You recall with a newly alien memory
The war in heaven, the loss of the seventh star,
And the terror of dark, unbearable densities.

Awakened without time to find your mind in the dark,
You cannot tell were you angel or devil in that flight.
From something to do with the body you feel the brain
Honestly trying to make conventional sense
Of the paranoid codes that tap insistently
With pinyon branches on the metal roof.
It is so late at night that even Milton
Would seem a reading of the evening news.
They are out there all right, passing
Easily through everything that comes their way.
What you don't hear is how they strike you
Hollow of sleeping body, so it best takes soul,
Or a templated mind wiped clean of thoughts
And emptied of the senses noise and imagery.
Like telescopes away from city lights,
Only the deepest dreamless sleep provides
The minimum of existence that is still
Thin film enough to catch the life of stars.
This music takes a mind with no one in it.

II. FASTNACHT, BERN, MARCH 7, 1987

(For Ralph)

We, on the other side of dreamless sleep,
Still live out wholly unknown enormous
Intangent, galactically extended lives;
And we're not supposed to know otherwise.
If only for one night I'd like to be
Other-wise, to see undark and entire
Eros, to look back at Eurydice
To know what other god she beds down.
Earth's flowers cannot twist to see their stems,
Even our moon has its darkness all turned out,
And mind is strapped to know what god intends
On riding the saddle of our time-bound thought.
In the night-time half is there another half,
Nesting like those painted Russian dolls?
Then each half could contain another whole
Half-life relatively timed in fractals.
Well, there's Einstein's House across the street,
And here's the crowd in which I am content
To say farewell to flesh, hello to Lent,
Unmasked, ordinary, not even indiscreet.
If each half of a half is never breached,
For all the other lives inside of me,
Then each creature dreams asymptotically
Until fractal infinity is finely reached.
Coiled in the smallest possible fragments spring,
Abundant in every dream-drenched sod
-den piece of life becoming everything,
The brute fact possible remains of God.
In other words, we're everybody every night
And live all the lives there are at once,
Rich man, poor whore, wise man, and dunce,

And only then come dumb again in light.
When we finally guess who we really con
It's bound to be good for a good long laugh;
Small wonder we like carnival's riff-raff,
Pretending with masks to put each other on.

III. WORLDS INTERPENETRATING AND APART

(For Francisco)

The inexplicable beginning of worlds
Required gods in the air, germs in the sea,
Or else there was nothing held to explain,
Alone among causes, the greatest of old.
Albrecht Dürer and Hieronymus Bosch,
I think I am beginning to understand.
Worlds interpenetratingly apart
I remark, and mark here again in ink.
Angels, I observe, Greek and Hebraic,
Were messengers of old, unseen by all
Save the most artistic, imaginative
Women and men whose souls wore out holes
In their shod bodies until they were eyes.
Tied to the stake with martyr's eyes buried
Alive in their darkening flesh, they could see
Infinitesimal crystalline forms,
Now thought to be viruses, better known
As plagues, marks of the apocalypse, aids
To understanding the deadly sifting
Of sudden unbecoming worlds torn apart
Like Dürer's paper sky of martyrdom.
I confess to angels as viruses,
Elementals and gnomes, bacteria,
And plagues the final judgment for ending
The adaptive habits of the settled world.
But angels are not viruses only,
These the merest tip of penetration
In our world of bodies that know others
And while remaining a part of each
Equally, elsewhere also take their life.

IV. FOOD CHAINS

(For Lynn)

Chemical elements and bacteria make
Eighty percent of our body's weight.
Properly speaking these don't belong to us,
But if properly stripped of them, we'd die,
Unable to digest our food or rid
Ourselves of poisons. So, who do we think we are?
And why do we have to think it stops with us?
Say rather we're all anaerobes at heart,
Blindly alive in the dark guts of demons,
And all the rot of our fervent stinking emotions
Is only the gas given off to break down
Brutal matter to feed demented minds.
But who am I to say? Still, I like
To think. And one thing's certain and that is
Those demons don't like independent thoughts.
Patriotic seizures and possessed tribal wars,
Or perfectly murderous absolute *isms*:
These the feed lots they like to keep us in.
A thought without hatred is indigestible to them,
For they cannot make conglomerate bodies above
The light reflecting surface of a mind.
They prefer more noisy urban incarnations.
And so we have Muzak everywhere:
The refrigerator's calming hum that keeps us
Mindless in tune with the herd of human flesh
And stops us from spoiling before their meal.
It's easy to find demons in great numbers
Above stock markets in panic, British
Soccer games, battles, Heavy Metal clubs,
Secret police stations and special brothels
Built to extrude bodies held to torture.

Epilogue

It goes on, for these gaseous demons
that hover above our wretched intensities are food
For more Olympian gods who take delight
In entire epochs and stretch out in time
Whole human civilizations as their feast.
All myths are true but literally mis-taken:
Odors of sacrifice do delight real gods,
And crafty aliens and little green men
Move in and out of multiplied dimensions,
Overlapping worlds that are tightly packed
Like the coils of our guts in which germs thrive.
They say there are stars that stuff black holes,
Do you think God gets a big bang out of it?

V. ORIGINS OF LIFE

(For Lynn)

Say, Oracle, how life first came to Earth.
Did lightning strike the prebiotic sea,
And ditch electric wonders to soft clay beds;
Or did life spring from hot submarine vents,
Below the ultra waved surface of light?
Speak again of emergent properties,
Of how Gaia could no longer bear the seed
Of Ouranos and called to her crime-born sons
To cut his balls off and cast them streaming
With blood and semen into the wine-dark sea.
These things are unspeakable, therefore sing.
Scientists they say are speakers for things,
But how can they know or say, and what
Is a thing? Things are never known, they are
The remains of thought, like love stains on sheets.
Because of all their things we choke in cities
And the forests with whom man lately evolved
Die from the exhaustions of unspeakable acts.
Scientists say that flowers and hominids
Appeared, emerged, evolved together;
Small wonder that poets remarked the spring
As now they do the unwild death of trees.
In famines in Africa the young die first,
Massacre of the innocents whose swollen eyes
Are empty of belief. What must the trees think
Of science that will not speak of the end of worlds
But leaves that to crazies who sign the streets.
Say again Oracle of the ends and origins
Of things. Let mind return to its primal source
Intimately in the cunnilingual night,
Linger in the oestral redolent odor, listen

To ancient pheromones and speak with tongues.
Angels I think may have taken sleeping advantage
Of me. And I can live with that, though I find
They leave no traces except for alien thoughts
That were not there when I went alone to bed.
I think I begin to know how women feel.
They too are scientists of an archaic kind
That can read moon stains on sunlit sheets.
Light is too harsh for that internal flesh.
Yes, that must have been the place of origin,
Where magma cracked and earth gave vent to life,
As the first membrane allowed by distant light
Enclosed the mess and message of the cell.
I begin to know how women feel, but would,
If only science would give way to you,
Still know how worlds end in rotting air.

VI. THE SHAPE OF THE WORLD

(For Jim)

Die Welt ist alles, was der Fall ist.
Die Welt ist die Gesamtheit der Tatsachen, nicht der Dinge.
Die Welt is durch die Tatsachen bestimmit und dadurch,
dass es alle Tatsachen sind.
>   Ludwig Wittgenstein,
>   *Tractatus Logico-Philosophicus*

I.
The World
The World is
The World is all
The World is all that is
The World is all that is the Fall.

II.
The World is the entirety
of the actually known,
and not the collection of things.

III.
The World is
through actualities
decided,
and through these
that it is
all the actualities.

IV.
What we ignore
rages out
and in outrage begins
another world.

V.

Worlds are not containers of things.
The innocent think that there are facts
out there in space, waiting to be
proved and set upon a shelf.
The guilty know better and have watched
their cunning minds in disbelief
commit casual atrocities.

VI.

Worlds embrace repulsions.
The fiercest rejections stitch
the whole together, stabbing
to release blood and gas;
no matter how foul, it serves
to feed one life with another.
Life pollutes, and worlds
are made whole of it.
Blue-green algae eat light
and excrete oxygen
that kills the little buggers
that were here before we ever
got round to sex and death.

VII.

We speak with stricken tongues, stains
upon the shattered flesh of trees,
but chemistry goes under speech
to touch, and hum, and musically lick
the electrical skin of molecules.
So worlds end erotically
as they began, with death sucking
the life out of erected stars.
It was for good archetypal reasons
that the Victorians called wet dreams
pollution, for they undoubtedly had
carnal knowledge of the death of stars.

VII. THE END OF WORLDS

(For Jim)

Pollution is truly economic,
a new medium of exchange,
in which conflicted worlds arise
like deadly excreted coral reefs.
Hiroshima, Bikini Atoll,
Seveso, Bhopal, Chernobyl,
L.A., Osaka, and Detroit:
the dulling air grows unintelligible
to the brains of damaged children
and the brittle tendrils of conifers,
but the machines are not disturbed.
As robots replace workers,
the punks decorate the streets
and sign off with agonic displays
left over from the older animal world.
Infolded with innumerable extinctions,
Life gathers the species to itself,
like kneaded dough punched down
to let out the distending gas
and rise half-baked again.
From cell to plant to animal
to human, and now to God knows what.
Lynn says a planet of machines.
Jim says another age of ice,
and I believe him.
I think only those Taoist mystics,
transformed by a future Chinese science,
will be able in smaller numbers
to survive the Artificial Intelligence
of their American machines
in which viruses replace silicon and men

become little organelles.
As mitochondria once
moved into the cell, so now men
will turn to noetic circuitry
on Earth and extended Space.
Time's pure intelligible Beings,
Angels again as of old on high
will encircle the electronic Earth
and take light body in the softest ware,
in those untaught lines
of topology and chaotic grace
that you can see arising now
in the dragon fractaled clouds
or on the playful, Peano curving,
surface of the swiftest river Aare.
There will be,
for those not taken up
into the rest of understanding
in the mathematical world,
far fewer of us required
in those warm equatorial belts
of easy Gaian Ice Age Life,
fewer to serve the vessels
in which mankind survived.
Once anaerobes abounded,
now they sulk in our guts,
and so it will be
with what is left of us.
Once animals roamed at will,
now they are contained
as evolutionary artifacts
on the Serengeti Plain.
From Australian aborigine
to New York arbitrage broker,
nothings seems ever lost;
each stage is held organelle

within the planetary noetic Cell.
The posthuman world
is probably unimaginable
and likely not all that bad.
Of that which we cannot speak,
Wittgenstein said we should be silent,
but perhaps we are allowed to sing
in the sharp consolation of art,
quaintly out of tune,
alone, alien in Bern,
staring out the rear window
to the glaciers of the Jungfraujoch,
and imagining in the Alpine night
the growing immortal ice
taking its own good time
to still our lovely, swift, jade green Aare.

VIII. THE LESSONS OF HISTORY

(For Ralph)

When hunters and gatherers roamed
in their seasonal rounds,
for those windowless nomads,
it was Evil to settle down,
to stop time or try to take count
of what one person had.
It was indeed woman
that brought man fruits and grains,
the things that needed to be
contained in breast-shaped pots,
or ground on heavy stones.
So the man settled for less
of the streams and wandering sky
by accepting the offer of more
in turning the earth to dirt.
Then things began to count.
We call this History,
or the First Mentality
of lunar enumeration.
The spotless women kept track
of moons as they had before,
but the men grew uneasy
and found their own new cults
of blood in raids and war
more fascinating than
the wound that monthly heals
itself and gives new life.
Death began to matter
when people took on names
and acquired property.
As cities began to shape,
so did the lines of numbers

corner to geometry.
From Egypt to ancient Greece,
things began to shapen up
in the perfect state of rest.
For the ancients, motion
was imperfect, hence Evil,
the Fall into matter and time.
Thus they wrote it down
in the Second Mentality.
But Galileo, Newton,
Leibniz and Descartes
looked on falling bodies
and found them surprisingly good.
Plato's eternal circles,
saving their appearances,
had only one point to make,
but Kepler's elliptical laws
of planetary motion
required a second point
that dynamically began
to make more sense to us.
So this how we moderns
began to form in lines
of linear equations
in the Third Mentality.
We now of this set of mind
find noise and chaos almost
vampiric in its Evil.
But our children don't.
Watch them do their homework
with their Sony headphones on.
They ghettoblast the streets
and break dance circles
round square geometry.
They make huge fun with numbers
in hard rock festivals,

and the louder it can get
the better it sounds to them.
Our children look upon Evil
and the loss of their hearing
in discotheques and clubs
and find it unnaturally Good.
So now in higher math,
chaos is termed attractor,
and sexuality
the basin that sucks us in.
So here we go again
to the Fourth Mentality.
But this is the Big One
that can jive all the rest:
arithmetic geometries
that dynamically dance apart
in chaotic topologies.
The unholy philosophers
who tore our minds apart
themselves were sacrificed
in the clearing of the void:
syphilitic Nietzsche,
hack Nazi Heidegger,
and even AIDS-stricken
Michel Foucault, were right.
It is "The End of Man."
"We came too late for the gods,
and too soon for Being."
Now slowly the forests die,
the ozone layer thins out,
while the brown seas thicken
like dusk in Tuscany.
The bright new computers
with their terminal disease
give us aborted births,
cataracts and glaucoma.

Life dies exactly timed
to the spread of our machines.
We are indeed off when we think
the computers are not on to us.
Yeats was right, the beast
slouches to be born,
but has no need of us
to slip in our sullen flesh.
In the past, Mind found itself
gelatinously in cells,
and that got Gaia going;
now the Evil Demiurge
as Ahriman and Rock
has better things to do.
No need to harken back
out of step in cloven hoof
and batty leathern wings,
behold the microchip,
the new amorphous crystal
and superconducting clay.
Adam is remade again
in a better sort of mud.
A shudder in the lattice
engenders there the burning
rockets and the air gone dead.
Oh, we will survive all right
in our descendants as now
do crocodiles and lizards,
recalling dinosaurs;
but once the Mind has moved
from basic carbon Life,
we will scarcely linger on
in the shadows of ourselves.
So pollution is in timing,
along with everything else,
to take us as fast away

as the lattice comes in play.
The Fundamentalists
in "Rapture" are almost there;
in their white trash heaven,
they can personally see
no limit to their credit;
not the Daimonic Mind
that watches how and what
we feel when we take life
in a body and out.
At this inhuman level
it can't be politics,
of the decent sort that thinks
it can clean up the air,
put out the poor to use,
end all wars, Stop AIDS,
and even unemployment.
In their own crazy way,
the paranoid myths are not
half-bad in the good they do
as epistemological cartoons.
The end of the world is here,
and the body-snatchers too.
Nothing is much the same,
and cults are a kind of quick take
for busy airport people
who haven't got the time
quite right; I guess that's why
we still have need of art.
Anyway, that's only half
the planetary story.
Evil and noise are merely
inhuman instruments.
Just as we hit that drum
and strike strung guts with bows,
so does this Evil conspire

only to serve the Fifth
Mentality of Time.
So out of computer chips
and satellited nets
the last noise about us
escapes to evolving sound.
Whatever woven bodies
they might later take,
has all been told before:
In Bach's B Minor Mass,
the *Sanctus* is the space
that time prepared for us.

INDEX

193

INDEX

Index

Index